COGNOS 8 BI

FOR CONSUMERS

COGNOS 8 BI
FOR CONSUMERS

A step-by-step
introductory
guide to
Cognos
Connection

Juan A. Padilla
Technology Partners Books

Cognos 8 BI for Consumers

A step-by-step introductory guide to Cognos Connection

By Juan A. Padilla

For information, contact:

Technology Partners Books, PMB #378, 1353 Road #19, Guaynabo, PR, USA 00966

Email: info@technologypartnersbooks.com

Web: www.technologypartnersbooks.com

All terms mentioned in this book that are known to be trademarks have been appropriately capitalized.

Every effort has been made to make this book as complete and as accurate as possible. The author and the publisher assume no responsibility for errors or omissions, or for damages resulting from the use of the information contained herein.

ISBN: 978-0-9796920-0-0

Book editor: Lisa Taylor Huff, www.LisaTaylorHuff.com

Cover Image © 2007 Jupiterimages Corporation

Models are for illustrative purposes only.

FIRST EDITION

Dedication

To my wife Dorka Marie for her patience;

To my daughters Sharazad and Keyla Marie for their understanding;

And to all my family for being so special.

About the Author

Juan A. Padilla has been developing Cognos Business Intelligence solutions for the last 10 years. With an extensive background in database management working with companies such as Oracle, IBM and Scientech, Padilla has mastered the integration of technology with business needs. He is co-founder of Technology Partners, Inc., an information technology (IT) company that focuses on Business Intelligence, Custom Software Development and Database Administration where he presently works as Solution Architect defining complex IT solutions for leading worldwide organizations.

Table of Contents

1

Chapter 1: Introduction

Business Intelligence, or BI for short, is the process of transforming raw data from systems, databases, files and other sources into powerful information that can be leveraged in making business decisions. By applying the power of BI tools to your company's raw data, you enable that data to help your organization analyze trends, to see how a particular product line is selling, to determine market share, to compare your products to a competitor's, and to give you the critical information you need to forecast and make informed decisions in your business.

With millions of users worldwide, Cognos is, without a doubt, a leading provider of Business Intelligence tools. Their latest release, **Cognos 8 BI,** is a powerful suite of modules that share a common infrastructure for the creation, management and deployment of queries, reports, analyses, scorecards, dashboards and alerts (we will refer to these as BI Objects). User roles manipulate these BI objects by utilizing components of Cognos 8 BI. Those roles and components will be the topic of this introductory chapter.

So, welcome to *Cognos 8 BI for Consumers*, a step-by-step introductory guide to **Cognos Connection**—the standard portal of Cognos 8 BI. As the first in a series of books on Cognos 8 BI, this guide concentrates on the basics and fundamentals required by Cognos 8 BI users at all levels.

How this book came to be

I am a former Oracle employee. (Nowadays, everyone seems to be). I spent over eight years working with its technology, and in my opinion, the Oracle database technology was wonderful, but its analysis (multidimensional) database could have been improved. Therefore, when I, along with a few peers, started my own company in 1998 to provide Oracle services, we looked for complementary technologies to enhance the available functionality of the Oracle database. That is when we stumbled upon Cognos.

Cognos has been around a long time, at least by information technology standards. They have been in business since the early 1970s, first doing consulting work and then transitioning to software development and business intelligence tools. Their website (www.cognos.com) provides a detailed timeline of their history. (Of course, I have also been around since the early '70s, but in my case, I was barely starting to walk!)

So, when we evaluated Cognos, we discovered that they had some nice tools for reporting and analyzing, called Impromptu and PowerPlay. The tools focused on business users, enabling them to create ad hoc queries, reports and analyses with just a few mouse clicks. Of course, there was some background work that had to be done to make the tools user friendly, but Cognos' development tools were powerful; and because we were a consulting company, we saw Cognos as a good business opportunity. Thus, we decided to establish a partnership and started to promote the Cognos technology.

This turned out to be a great decision! Today, Cognos has come a long way and has built a strong reputation for visionary technology and powerful business solutions. I am certain that this year they will join the dozen-or-so other independent software companies that can boast revenues of over $1 billion—quite an exclusive club.

With a clear vision of the future, Cognos decided in the early years of the new millennium to completely rewrite their solutions, using pure web technologies with a single infrastructure for their entire suite of products. In 2003, they launched Cognos ReportNet, a very powerful, HTML-only query and reporting tool. That was the beginning of a constant rewriting of their family of products until the latest version, Cognos 8 BI, into which they have now integrated their query, reporting, analyses, scorecarding, dashboarding and event management tools into a single architecture with shared components. Cognos 8 BI is an extremely powerful solution that has evolved (and continues to evolve) into a fully integrated Corporate Performance Management tool, through which an organization can not only evaluate its past performance, but constantly monitor its present behavior and, even better, plan for the future.

Because I have used Cognos products for the last 10 years and have even been an instructor for most of their courses, I have constantly had requests from friends, peers and customers to teach them about Cognos. Of course, I was delighted to do it, but with a new child at home and major client projects at work, it was becoming more difficult and time-consuming to personally teach each person who asked. That compelled me to write a Cognos review to support those who seemed to need it. Several pages later, that review became a booklet, and it kept growing until I ended up with this book (and the realization that what was really needed was an entire *series* of Cognos tutorial books).

Instead of a book, I prefer to call this a visual step-by-step guide. It is the closest to a personalized tutorial I can provide without physically being in the room with you. The guide relies heavily on screenshots that demonstrate the workflow and the available features Cognos offers.

Most of the people who ask me for help with Cognos have not yet installed or used Cognos products, but want to learn for multiple reasons. Therefore, I created this guide for

- those who are evaluating Cognos and want a better understanding of the available capabilities;

- those who may soon be using Cognos products, e.g. those seeking a new job or those looking for consulting opportunities;

- those who already use previous versions of Cognos and need to evaluate the current functionality in depth, in order to make decisions about application upgrades and migrations;

- and, of course, those novice users who are just now starting to use Cognos products, for whom this guide can serve as a reference source to be used any time, anywhere.

This completes how I came to write this book. I hope you enjoy the guide, and that is useful in teaching you what you want and need to know about the Cognos 8 BI environment.

About This Book

Cognos 8 BI for Consumers is the first in a series of books I am writing on Cognos technology. This book will focus on the Consumer role (we will discuss "roles" shortly) which provides the base functionality of Cognos 8 BI. The base capabilities are expanded by adding additional modules, called Studios; for example, one Studio adds ad hoc query capabilities to a Consumer role, another Studio adds analysis features, and yet another adds scorecarding functionality, and so on. You only buy, install and configure the Cognos modules you really need, rather than pay for functionality you will not use.

Thus, this introductory guide focuses on topics relevant to the infrastructure available to *all* Cognos 8 BI users, including:

- Learning to use the available functionality of Cognos Connection, the standard Cognos 8 BI portal;

- Working with reports, including execution, scheduling, setting parameters and switching formats;

- Customizing the look and feel of the portal through user preferences;

- Simulating working with security to learn those features; and

- Exploring multiple report samples and the powerful reporting possibilities in Cognos 8 BI.

The book is based on the latest available release at the time it was written: Cognos 8 BI version 8.2. Some functionality has necessarily been excluded from discussion because of timing issues with the release of the software versions and this guide's publication; especially important is the absence of the Cognos Go! family of interfaces that are currently in a branding and technical transition.

This guide is not intended to be a complete replacement for Cognos Documentation; on the contrary, it serves as a complement to the official documentation and provides a different teaching approach.   Most highly detailed information is still available only in the Cognos Documentation.

Assumptions

By following the screenshots provided you will be able to grasp the functionality of Cognos 8 BI; however, if you are actually doing the hands-on step-by-step process, you will also need to have:

- Basic web browsing experience;

- Access to Cognos 8 BI 8.2 through a web browser, preferably in an environment where security has not yet been enabled (by default, when you install Cognos 8 BI, there is no security defined, which allows you to have access to all functions for testing or training purposes.   Configuring Cognos security is an advanced topic that will not be covered extensively in this book).

- Installed and configured sample databases and packages included with the Cognos 8 BI software.

Getting Started with Cognos 8 BI

Now that you know the history behind the book and what to expect, let us get into Cognos 8 BI by reviewing the requirements of different types of users of Cognos 8 BI, and how they can be related to the specific tools they will use.

Cognos 8 BI

Cognos 8 BI is a powerful suite of products that focuses on transforming raw data into powerful information for business decisions.   Cognos 8 BI can be used across all levels in an organization, from users looking for pre-defined reports to analysts with complex data requirements.   For all levels of users, Cognos 8 BI has a tool.

User Roles

The users of Cognos 8 BI can be grouped into four major roles based upon their respective business and technical requirements.   These groups include the following:

- **Consumers** – are users who want to have access to pre-defined content.   Most of the time, they want to access the content through a web portal, but in some scenarios they may require access to content from MS Office, by performing searches, or through a mobile device such as a Blackberry.

- **Authors** – are power users who have access to advanced tools to create and maintain ad hoc queries, reports, analyses, scorecards, dashboards and alerts.   They build the BI objects that will later be accessed by the Consumers.

- **Developers** – have access to development tools that build the infrastructure required by Authors to develop content.   They create user-friendly layers used by Cognos 8 BI studios for Authors to use.

- **Administrators** - have access to configuration, administration and monitoring tools to ensure the availability and performance of the Cognos 8 BI infrastructure.

These four roles use a combination of Cognos 8 BI modules to perform their work.

Cognos 8 BI Modules

The Cognos Business Intelligence solution is divided into multiple components with specific functionality to support the previously defined roles.

Consumer Modules

Consumers utilizing pre-defined content from Cognos 8 BI use the following modules. By pre-defined content, we mean queries, reports, analyses, scorecards, dashboards and alerts already developed by Authors and made available for use by those in Consumer roles.

- **Cognos Connection** - is the Cognos 8 BI standard portal that provides a single point of access to all Business Intelligence objects. The user can have access to public and personal folders where he or she can execute reports, access queries, view analyses, monitor scorecards and execute monitoring agents. From Cognos Connection, the user is able to access and browse content, see properties, assign permissions, and schedule objects, among other tasks.

- **Cognos Go!** - is a new family of alternative interfaces *(These are quickly evolving and may have changed dramatically by the time this book is published)*:

  - **Go! Office** - is a tool that allows access to Cognos 8 BI content from MS Office tools, such as Excel, Word and PowerPoint.

  - **Go! Search** - is a powerful search engine integrated into Cognos 8 BI that allows quick searches—not only on BI objects stored in the Cognos Connection portal, but on data used *by* those objects.

  - **Go! Mobile** - allows access to Cognos BI objects through mobile devices, such as Blackberries. Go! Mobile will automatically adjust the object to the device, so it will be highly optimized for the features available on each.

Author Modules

The following modules, called Studios, are used by Authors to develop content for Consumers.

- **Query Studio** - is a very user-friendly ad hoc query tool that allows users to easily access information. With Query Studio, the user drags and drops fields to execute queries, and with multiple available options at a touch of the mouse, it can group data, create summaries, display charts, filter information and export data. An Author who has access to Query Studio is referred to as a **Business Author**.

- **Metrics Studio** - is a powerful scorecard tool that allows for the creation and monitoring of goals through an organization. An Author who has access to Metrics Studio is a **Business Manager**.

- **Analysis Studio** - is the user-friendly tool used to quickly analyze summarized information with powerful dimension and variable crossing for complex analysis, discovery of trends and forecasting. An Author who has access to Analysis Studio is a **Business Analyst**.

- **Report Studio** – is the professional report-authoring tool. The tool allows for the development of pixel-perfect reports, such as invoices and statements, as well as very complex layouts, such as those required for enterprise dashboards. An Author who has access to Report Studio is a **Professional Author**.

- **Event Studio** – is a monitoring tool that allows for the definition of agents that will monitor certain user-defined events and will execute tasks accordingly. They can be saved to Cognos as "agents". Event Studio access is included for Professional Authors.

Developer Modules

One of the most powerful features of Cognos 8 BI is the capability to encapsulate the complexity of multiple databases, exposing business information through a simple, easy to use layer. The following modules are used by Developers to create a user-friendly layer that Authors will use to create their content.

- **Framework Manager** – is a development tool to create the end-user layer used by Authors to build their BI objects.

- **OLAP Designer** – is a development tool used to model and create multidimensional databases. A multidimensional database, often referred to as a "cube", is a highly compressed database and contains summarized information that is optimized for analysis.

- **Metrics Designer** – is a development tool used to model and deploy scorecards and related data loading procedures.

- **Data Manager** – is a development tool commonly referred to as an ETL. ETL stands for Extraction, Transformation and Loading. It *extracts* data from multiple sources or systems; *transforms* or integrates it; and then *loads* it to a central database for use with BI tools.

Administrator Modules

The following modules are used by Administrators to configure, manage, monitor, optimize and troubleshoot a Cognos 8 BI installation.

- **Cognos Configuration** – is the Cognos 8 BI administrative tool that is used to define the behavior of a Cognos 8 BI installation. It is used to manage configuration parameters.

- **Cognos Connection** – is used to monitor, configure and optimize a Cognos 8 BI installation through a web interface. It is the same tool used by Consumers, but contains other advanced options for administration.

A Quick Tour

In the next chapter, you will have your first opportunity to see Cognos Connection in action. We will complete a quick-guided tour to familiarize you with how it works, some of the features that are available, and more.

2

Chapter 2: Cognos 8 BI Quick Tour

In this chapter, you will be led through a quick tour of Cognos 8 BI, which heavily focuses on Cognos Connection. Cognos Connection is the Cognos 8 BI standard portal solution. It allows users to configure personal preferences, navigate through public and private folders, and access Business Intelligence objects, such as queries, reports, analyses, scorecards, dashboards—all using a web-based environment.

Connecting to Cognos 8 BI

Cognos 8 BI is Cognos' suite of Business Intelligence products packaged with a common infrastructure. One of the components of the common infrastructure is Cognos Connection, a web-based portal; thus, much of the functionality available to Consumers is accessible through a web browser, although other interfaces are available for specific requirements, such as access through MS Office or a Blackberry mobile device.

> *Although this book is about the functionality available for Consumers, the other interfaces are part of Cognos Go!, a fairly new family of alternative interfaces that are quickly evolving based on user requirements and market conditions. Because it is still an evolving product, we have decided not to include Cognos Go! in this book.*

As we are concentrating on Cognos Connection, we need to use a web browser to access the available functionality. For Consumers, Cognos supports most web browsers, including MS Internet Explorer, Firefox, and Opera, among others. The complete list of supported web browsers is available at the Cognos Support site and is constantly updated to reflect new releases.

1. To connect to Cognos 8 BI, enter the specific URL address of your installation in the web browser. It should look something like: http://myserver.mydomain/cognos8

MS Internet Explorer – entering URL address to connect to Cognos 8 BI

Three common situations where the address will differ are:

- Using Cognos in a secured mode using SSL (Secure Sockets Layer). In this case, the URL will include "https" instead of "http" to denote the added level of security.
  - o ***https***://myserver.mydomain/cognos8
- Using a different communications port than the standard for the web server. The standard port is 80, so if an installation uses the default, it does not have to be specified. If you are using a non-standard port (i.e. 8080), the URL may look like:
  - o http://myserver.mydomain:***8080***/cognos8
- Using a different alias than the standard for Cognos 8 BI installation. The URL may look like:
  - o http://myserver.mydomain:8080/***c8bi***

Alternatively, you may need to use a combination of any of these. Check with your administrator for your correct URL address.

You will know it is working when see the Cognos 8 BI splash page, followed by the Cognos 8 BI Welcome Page.

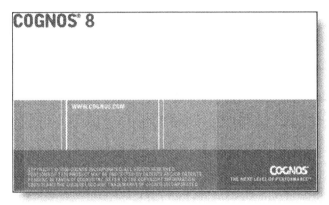

Cognos 8 BI – Splash page

Welcome Page

Cognos 8 BI provides an initial welcome page as the starting entry point. The page is intended as a launch pad for the Cognos tools to which a particular user has access. Based on security, the options displayed will vary depending upon the profile of the user connecting to the tool. The following Welcome Page shows all the available options.

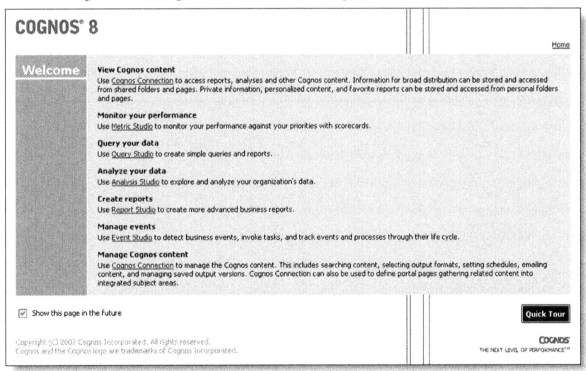

Cognos 8 BI – Welcome Page

Novice users who require a head start on the tool usually use the Welcome Page, which can be disabled at any time by deselecting the option "Show this page in the future" at the bottom of the page.

Here we can see the multiple options that are available, which we will discuss in more detail throughout this book. The Welcome Page shows us all the available options within Cognos 8 BI. Recapping the descriptions that appear on the Welcome Page, we can:

- **View Cognos content** – Use Cognos Connection to access reports, analyses and other Cognos content. Information for broad distribution can be stored and accessed from shared folders and pages. Private information, personalized content, and favorite reports can be stored and accessed from personal folders and pages.

- **Monitor your performance** – Use Metric Studio to monitor your performance against your priorities with scorecards.

- **Query your data** – Use Query Studio to create simple queries and reports.

- **Analyze your data** – Use Analysis Studio to explore and analyze your organization's data.

- **Create reports** – Use Report Studio to create more advanced business reports.

- **Manage events** – Use Event Studio to detect business events, invoke tasks, and track events and processes through their life cycle.

- **Manage Cognos content** – Use Cognos Connection to manage the Cognos content. This includes searching content, selecting output formats, setting schedules, emailing content, and managing saved output versions. Cognos Connection can also be used to define portal pages that gather related content into integrated subject areas.

Although the Consumer role is a base role that is also used by other more feature-rich roles, for the moment we are going to show Cognos Connection without security enabled, so users of all Cognos 8 BI roles will become familiar with the bigger picture. In the last chapter, we will discuss security in more detail and will be able to show what the interface will look like for a Consumer-only role.

Let us continue to the Cognos 8 BI portal so we can study the options in detail.

2. Select the Cognos Connection option (circled below) to access the Cognos 8 BI portal.

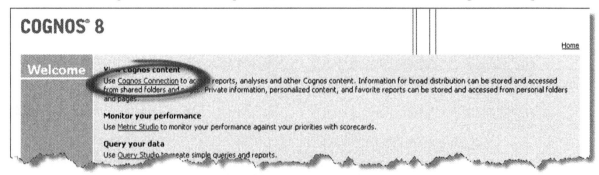

Access Cognos Connection from Welcome Page

You are now at Cognos Connection.

A first look at Cognos Connection

Cognos Connection is the Cognos 8 BI standard web-based portal. It contains all the objects that are available to users and provides access to all authoring and administrative components of Cognos 8 BI from a central location.

> *You may see some differences between the screenshots shown in the book and how Cognos Connection appears on your computer. Cognos 8 BI lets you personalize your portal (and we will show you how, later in the book). We personalized ours to make the images easier to read and print in our guide.*

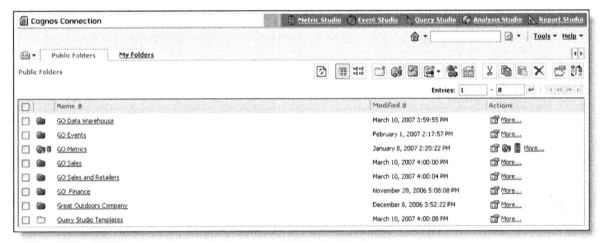

Cognos Connection – Initial page

> *If you see no entries, ask your administrator to set up the sample databases and packages included with the Cognos 8 BI software.*

The format shown is the standard out-of-the-box look and feel. It can be configured through preferences, cascading style sheets (CSS) and XML files to provide a customized experience, which is especially useful for integration with enterprise-wide portals, OEM systems and other business applications.

Executing a Report

I strongly believe that it is easier to learn by doing rather than by reading, so we will now begin to use the Cognos 8 BI functionality. Keep in mind that you may not be familiar with some of the options we will use, but rest assured that they will be discussed later on.

First, we need to find the report that we want to execute. From the Tab Navigator (see the file tabs in the upper left area of the page?) we can explore the options available. There is a list of folders on the Public Folders tab. The report that we want to execute is located in the Great Outdoors Company folder, so we have to navigate through this folder for access to our report.

3. Click on Great Outdoors Company (circled below) to see the additional content contained in the folder.

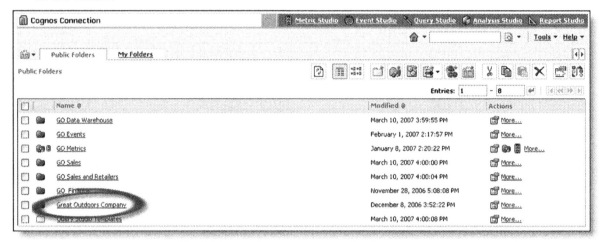

Public Folders – Navigate to Great Outdoors Company

By clicking the link, we can open and view the content of the Great Outdoors Company folder. Note that near the top, just below the Public Folders tab, the page displays our location in the hierarchy of folders, better known as the **navigation path**. (In the view shown below, the current path is Public Folders > Great Outdoors Company.) There are three folders available to us here. Our report is within the Report Studio Report Samples folder.

4. Click on Report Studio Report Samples (circled below) for a list of available reports in that folder.

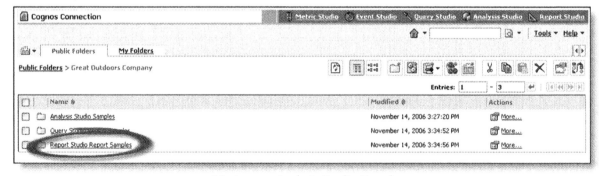

Navigate to Analysis Studio Samples

Now we can see the content of the Report Studio Report Samples folder. There are a number of objects with several icons. We will call these **Cognos BI reports.**

5. Click on "Revenue by Product Line" (circled below) to execute this report.

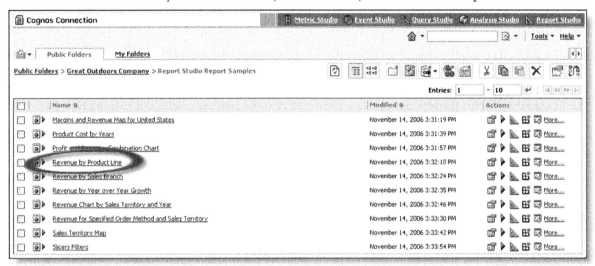

Click on a report to execute it

The report is then executed, and displays the corresponding output.

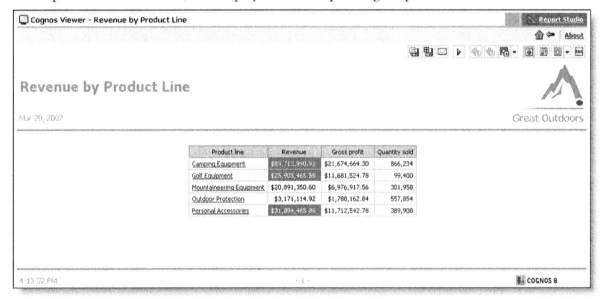

Shows an HTML report

Our report shows Revenue, Gross Profit and Quantity Sold by Product Lines. Three products with more than $25M in Revenue are highlighted.

You have now learned the basic and very easy process of accessing the Cognos Connection portal as well as executing a report! This is the same procedure Consumers will follow to execute any of their reports.

Next Steps

In subsequent chapters, we will delve into detail with Cognos Connection's features and functions. There are many additional features that make the Cognos Connection an important component of the Cognos 8 BI suite of tools. These features provide a common infrastructure for all Cognos 8 BI modules and ensure a standard, user-friendly look and feel that provides users with incredible ease of use without a major learning curve.

3

Chapter 3: Understanding the Interface

In this chapter, we will progress deeper into the interface functionality of Cognos Connection. We will learn the basics of the interface and learn more about several of the fundamental options, such as search and help.

Understanding Cognos Connection

Cognos Connection is the most important interface for users of Cognos 8 BI. With Cognos Connection as a starting point, we have most of the Cognos 8 BI functions available to us in a pure HTML interface. Cognos Connection is used by Consumers looking for specific queries, reports, analyses, dashboards or alerts, by Authors that create them, and by Administrators that monitor and manage them; thus it is a single interface with multiple uses.

After the initial Welcome Page (which can be disabled at any time) is the portal page of Cognos 8 BI, which is the main entrance to all other functions and features available in the system.

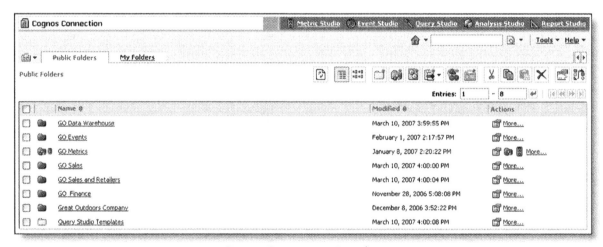

Cognos Connection – Initial page

The format shown above is the standard, out-of-the box look and feel. Later, we will discuss how to change that look and feel by applying templates. We will also describe how to change the initial page so that instead of seeing the Public Folders, we are able to see more relevant business information for our needs, such as a Business Monitoring Dashboard we can use as our customized Welcome Page.

Cognos Connection Initial Page Components

The page can be broken down into three major sections:

- The Studio Toolbar
- The Utilities Toolbar
- The Tab Navigator

Let us take a closer look at each one.

The Studio Toolbar appears at the very top of the page. It allows access to the suite of BI authoring tools.

First section – Studio Toolbar

Metric Studio – used to monitor business performance by defining goals and tracking them against targets. Goals can be placed into groups called Scorecards.

Event Studio – used to monitor specific user-defined events and perform tasks accordingly.

Query Studio – used to perform ad hoc queries.

Analysis Studio – used to analyze information with powerful drill-down capabilities, slicing and dicing functionality and exploration options.

Report Studio – used to create reports, from simple lists and crosstabs to complex, highly formatted reports, such as invoices and statements.

The authoring options appear in the Studio Toolbar based on security permissions, and as we are not using security yet, all the options are available. These options are outside the scope of this book and will be focused upon in future books in this series.

The Utilities Toolbar allows access to utilities, such as search tools, advanced tools and help facilities. These are complementary options that help Consumers get more value from the Cognos Connection functionality.

Second section – Utilities Toolbar

The Tab Navigator appears below the Utilities Toolbar. It lets us navigate through multiple information pages. By default, only two tabs are shown: Public Folders and My Folders. Later, we will learn to add additional tabs containing more relevant information.

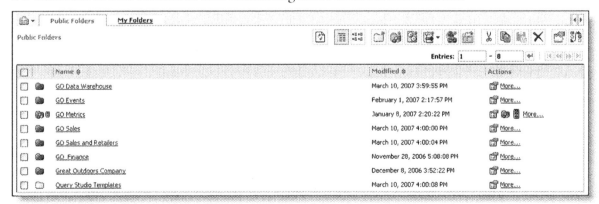

Third section – Tab Navigator

These three components are integrated into Cognos Connection, and the page's content varies based on security settings.

We will now discuss each toolbar in more depth.

Using the Studio Toolbar

As the base role, the Consumer does not have access to any of the Studios. The Studios will be covered in future books within this series. We currently see those options because we are using a default installation with the standard demonstration samples and without applying security. The toolbar is shown so that you can understand the integration of the Cognos 8 BI tools in the overall Cognos Connection portal.

Using the Utilities Toolbar

The Utilities are available from the second toolbar on the page and contain valuable functions that enhance our use of Cognos Connection. Let's discuss each option.

Home

The **Home** option is a quick way to return to your main page from deeper levels within the application.

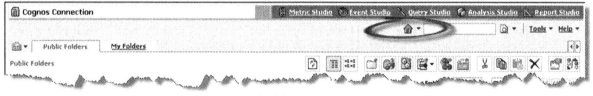

Go Home option

By clicking the Home icon (circled above), you can go to your designated Home page from any application section.

  Home - will take you to your designated Home page.

As you may notice, there is a small "down arrow" icon just to the right of the Home icon. The down arrow is an indication that a menu of more options is available and can be expanded for additional functionality.

▼   **Expand Menu** – shows additional available options for a menu.

1. Expand the Home menu by clicking the down arrow to the right.

Home menu

As we see, the drop-down menu contains two options:

Home   will take you to your designated Home page. It is equivalent to pressing the
                  Home icon.

Set View   will set up the Home option to point to your currently active Cognos
as Home   Connection page.

The Home options allow for fast navigation to a user-designated Home page. Therefore, if you navigate through the folders in Cognos Connection and get to a folder that you want to be your preferred or most-used folder, you can designate it as *your* "home" so you are able to navigate to it quickly in the future.

Searching for BI objects

The Search option (circled below) allows you to search for specific BI objects by Name, Description or both.

Search option

Search - will take you to the Search page, and will execute the search if you previously specified a value in the text box at the left of the option.

1. Expand the Search menu by clicking the down arrow to the right to show the available options.

Search menu

We see that the menu contains two options:

Search   will perform the same actions as selecting the Search icon.

Advanced   will take you to the Search page, but will display Advanced options for you to create complex search criteria.

2. Click on the Search option to get to the Search page.   The default Search page will provide functionality for executing a basic search on a Name, Description or both as specified on the Search options list. The default is to search for Name only.

Default Search page

If an advanced search is required, there is an "Advanced" option available as well. The advanced option will allow a user to filter the search by specifying additional criteria.

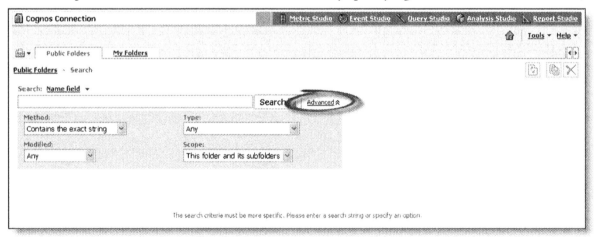

Advanced Search page

For our example, let us use the simple search.

3. Type in the search criteria of "product line" (you can leave out the double quotes) in the text box just beside the Search button, and press Search.

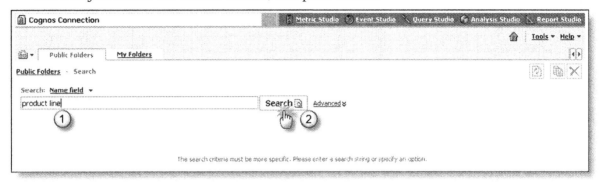

Specifying a search criteria

By executing a Search of those keywords, Cognos 8 BI will automatically provide a list of matching records. By browsing the search results, we can find our desired reports and execute them directly from the search results list.

4. Click on "Revenue by Product Line" to execute the particular report.

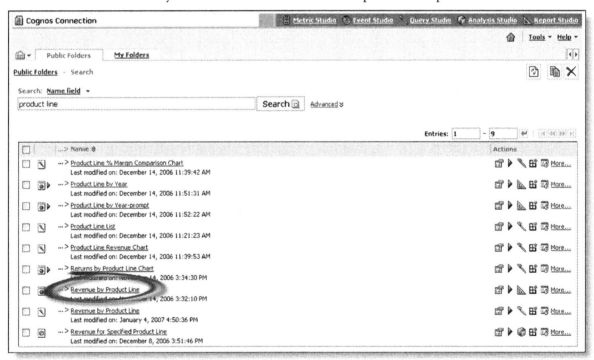

List of matching results

This should take you to the same "Revenue by Product Line" report that we executed previously. Therefore, instead of having to navigate through the folder structure in Cognos Connection for a report, which can prove tedious and time consuming if you are not sure where a specific report is located, you can use the Search option to find it quickly and easily!

Access to Advanced Tools

The next available option in the Utilities toolbar is Advanced Tools (circled below). These functions are available to multiple roles in Cognos 8 BI. In our case, we are going to focus only on those to which a Consumer has access, but will also provide a brief explanation of the others for your information.

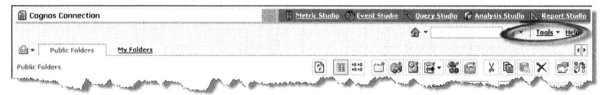

Tools option

When you select the Tools option, a menu will appear with several choices.

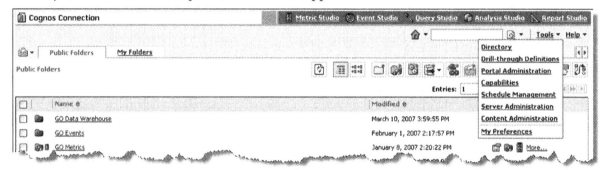

Tools menu

The options are:

Directory   This option allows for the configuration and maintenance of Security Roles and Groups, Data Source connections, Contacts and Distribution Lists and Printers. *This option is restricted by Cognos security and is not available to Consumers.*

Drill-through FOR CONSUMERS: Allows Consumers to browse through pre-
Definitions   defined drill-through definitions. Drill Through allows a Consumer to obtain additional information by transparently navigating from one report to another. The use of this option follows in the "Cognos Viewer" chapter, although the configuration is an advanced topic for a future book.

Portal   This option allows for the customization of the portal by modifying the
Administration standard look and feel based on business requirements. *This option is restricted by Cognos security and is not available to Consumers.*

Capabilities   This option allows administrators to control who has access to specific capabilities in Cognos 8 BI. Capabilities include access to the Studios and other advanced options, such as bursting, and administrative tools, among others. *This option is restricted by Cognos security and is not available to Consumers.*

Schedule Management	FOR CONSUMERS: This option allows Consumers to monitor and manage the scheduling of reports in Cognos 8 BI. Discussion of this option follows in the "Scheduling BI Objects" chapter.
Server Administration	This option allows administrators to monitor, manage and configure the Cognos 8 BI server infrastructure. *This option is restricted by Cognos security and is not available to Consumers.*
Content Administration	This option allows administrators to perform content backups and to migrate content from one system to another; for example, to deploy a new report from development to production. *This option is restricted by Cognos security and is not available to Consumers.*
My Preferences	FOR CONSUMERS: This option allows Consumers to personalize the look and feel of the Cognos 8 BI portal. In this option, the language of the portal, the colors and fonts, and the details that we see in the portal, among other options, can be configured. Discussion of this option follows in the "Customizing the Portal" chapter.

Getting Help

The last available option within the Utilities Toolbar is Help. Of course, Help is one of the first elements a new user needs to know. Cognos provides extensive documentation both in HTML and in PDF format. This documentation is available via the Help menu (circled below) in Cognos 8 BI.

Help option

When you expand the Help menu (click the down arrow to the right), several help options are presented.

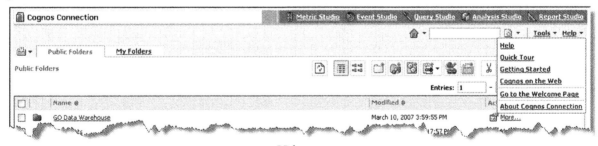

Help menu

You will find options to receive help in HTML and PDF formats, to access Cognos on the Web, to execute a basic tour of Cognos Connection, and to access other information, such as versions and programs installed.

Standard Help

The first option in the Help menu is to access the standard Help documents, which essentially comprise the Cognos 8 Administration and Security Guide manual in electronic format. The documents contain a wealth of information about using Cognos Connection, not just for Consumers, but also for Authors and Administrators.

1. Select the Help option (circled below) to access the Standard Help.

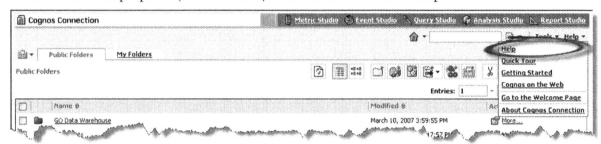

Accessing the Standard Help

The format is very user-friendly with options for Content, Index, Glossary, and Search. The Help is presented in an intuitive HTML format, enabling you to navigate via links.

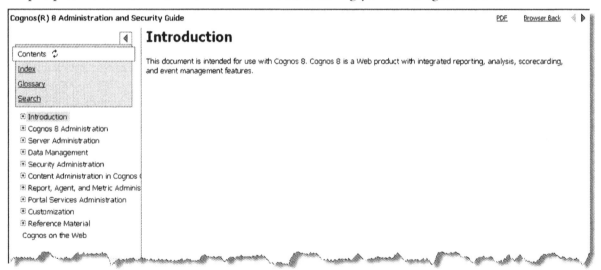

Help in HTML format

Help is also available as a PDF for those looking for a printer-ready format.

2. Click on the PDF option on the Help page (circled below).

Accessing the standard Help in PDF format

This will open a new window with the help file displayed in PDF format. Close the window to continue with the HTML format help. (Note: in order to view and print the help file in PDF format, you must have the **Adobe Acrobat Reader** installed on your computer. Visit **www.adobe.com** to download and install this software if you do not already have it; it is free!)

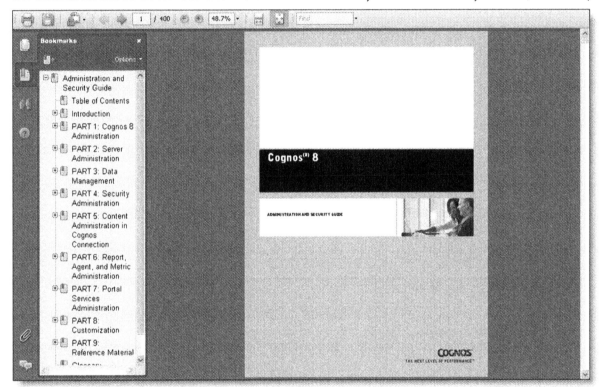

Help in PDF format

Close the PDF window to get back to the HTML format Help.

Looking once again at the HTML format, you can navigate through the Help file **Index**.

3. Click on the Index option (1) and select "changing Cognos 8 fonts" (2). Help information will display for that specific topic.

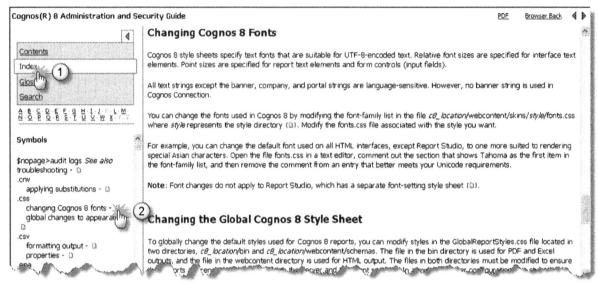

Using the Index functionality in the Standard Help

You can use the **Glossary** to look up common terms used in Cognos.

4. Click on the Glossary option (1) and select "anonymous access" (2) to view that topic.

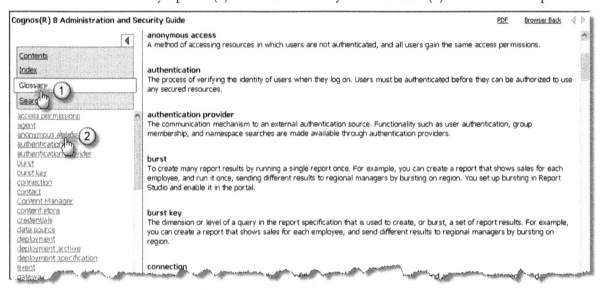

Using the Glossary functionality in the Standard Help

You can even **Search** for specific topics.

5. Click on the Search option (1), specify a term or keywords (2) in the search box (in this case, "help"), press the Search icon (3) and select from the search results (4) the result entitled "Using This Document".

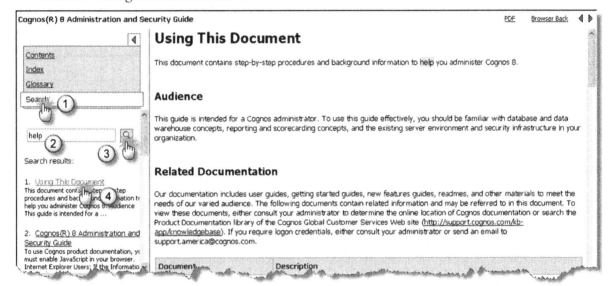

Using the Search functionality in the Standard Help

In summary, the standard help is quite useful and rich with features. Ideally, it could be improved by including more step-by-step examples and screenshots to help users follow along with instructions, but otherwise it is quite comprehensive.

Quick Tour

The second Help option is to access the Quick Tour, which presents an interactive animation of the Cognos 8 BI main functionality.

6. Select the Quick Tour option (circled below) from the Help menu.

Accessing the Quick Tour

The Quick Tour main page appears.

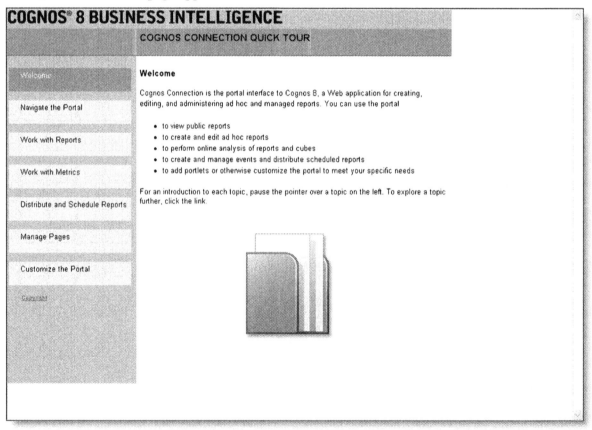

Cognos 8 BI Quick Tour

The Quick Tour is a very interactive introduction to Cognos Connection. Using the options shown, it enables users to discover Cognos 8 BI main features by simulating the navigation through the portal and executing multiple actions.

Getting Started

The third Help option is to access another document called Getting Started. This document provides a thorough overview of the different tools available for a novice user to learn and understand the Cognos solutions.

7. Select the Getting Started option to access the introductory Help.

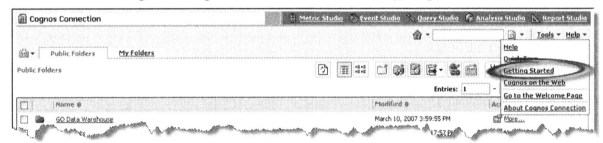

Accessing the Getting Started documentation

The option will show the Getting Started Page.

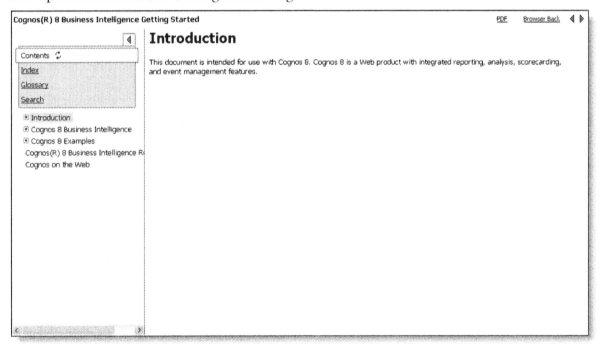

Cognos 8 BI Getting Started

The Getting Started feature provides a simple introduction to all Cognos 8 BI tools. If you are new to Cognos, it can help you understand the purpose of all the Cognos 8 BI modules, and it shows some step-by-step samples with images.

Getting Started uses the same user interface as Standard Help; thus, the Index, Glossary and Search features are also available. You can also access the PDF Help as shown above.

Cognos on the Web

The fourth option is to access the corporate Cognos web site. The Cognos site is well maintained and constantly updated, so it is a good idea to connect at least weekly to get the latest on Cognos news and events.

8. Select the Cognos on the Web option to access the corporate site.

Accessing the Cognos corporate site

This option will take you to the Cognos web site, which can also be accessed directly from any web browser at www.cognos.com.

> *If you are a Cognos customer, there is an option for Support in the Services menu on the Cognos web site. The Cognos Support site is top notch, with an excellent knowledge-based database, a case tracking system and download options for all Cognos software and documentation. I encourage you to take the time to visit the Cognos website and familiarize yourself with the Support they offer to their customers.*

Go to the Welcome Page

The fifth option is to access your Welcome Page.

9. Select the Go to the Welcome Page option to access the initial Cognos Connection page.

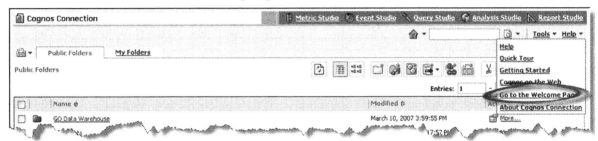

Accessing the Welcome Page

The option will show the pre-defined Welcome Page for the Consumer.

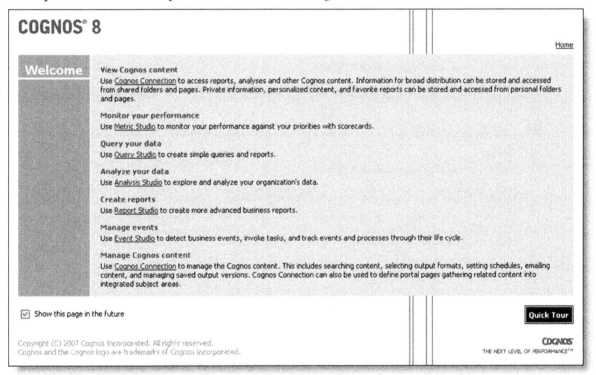

Default Welcome Page

Remember that the Welcome Page is tied to security, and based on your role, so it may show fewer options than those displayed here. In the Security chapter at the end of this book, we will show you a Consumer-only Welcome Page.

About Cognos Connection

The last option in the Help menu is to access information regarding the Cognos Connection installation.

10. Select the About Cognos Connection to access installation-related information.

Accessing About Cognos Connection information

The option will show data on the software version installed on your network or computer, as well as other important copyright information. If you are seeking technical support and need to do some troubleshooting, you may need to know the version of your release of Cognos; this is where you can find that information.

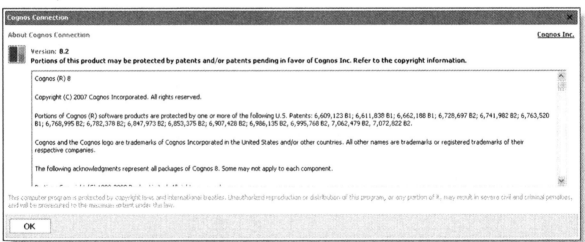

About Cognos Connection information

Using the Tab Navigator

The next chapter is dedicated to the Tab Navigator, the final component of the initial Cognos Connection page.

4

Chapter 4: Navigating through folders

Content in Cognos Connection is stored in folders, thus making them important organizational structures. This chapter focuses on navigating through folders and other functions available via the main toolbar of the Tab Navigator.

Introduction to Navigation in Cognos Connection

As soon as you connect to Cognos Connection (and pass the Welcome Page, if enabled), you will see the two main navigation "tabs" that show your storage options in the portal: Public Folders and My Folders. This is where all the Cognos 8 BI objects are stored within Cognos. The data and reports are accessible from your computer, but are physically stored on servers. Moreover, with the power of Cognos the information is available to you through a web browser.

This is actually a quite powerful feature as it allows you to have access to Cognos Connection content at anytime, from anywhere, provided you have access to a web browser that is able to connect to your Cognos 8 BI server (and provided you have the necessary privileges).

Public Folders Tab

Public Folders are designed to store content shared by multiple users. Sharing is done by applying security so only users with specific permissions are able to access the various items in the Public Folders.

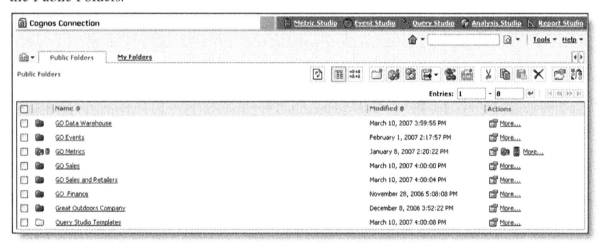

Cognos Connection initial page - Public Folders

When Consumers must share content, it is a common practice to create a folder structure to organize the information easily. Folders can be "nested" inside other folders, so the information can be grouped hierarchically using common business terms, such as departments or projects.

There are three main types of folders:

Standard Folder – this is a container for other folders and/or BI objects, and is used for organizational purposes. It will behave just like a folder on your local computer, but will operate like a web page with active links. A bright yellow icon specifies Standard folders.

Package Folder – this folder is similar to a Standard Folder, but internally it contains pre-defined business rules and metadata related to sources of information. It is used by the Studios to create new queries, reports, analyses, etc. A dark blue icon specifies Package folders.

 Metrics Folder – Metrics folders are used by the Metrics Studio to store metrics-related information. While the standard behavior upon selecting the other two folder types is to show their contents, a Metrics Folder will open up directly into Metrics Studio. A dark blue icon with colored dots specifies Metrics folders.

Throughout the examples that follow in this guide, we will focus on Standard and Package folders only; Metrics Folders will be discussed in the book for Business Managers.

My Folders Tab

In contrast to Public Folders, My Folders is used to keep BI objects private. It is used to store personal reports, queries, analyses, and scorecards, among other objects. In addition, it serves as temporary storage for BI objects in development and other "work in process" objects. For example, while creating a new report, a Power User may store the report in his or her My Folders area until it is ready for deployment; it would then be copied to Public Folders and security assigned accordingly.

Let us navigate to My Folders to study its content.

1. Select the My Folders tab to access the personal content.

Accessing My Folders

As you can see, the folder is empty. We do not have any personal content stored in My Folders... yet.

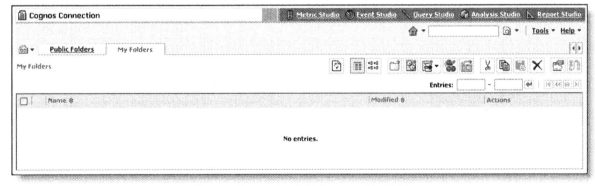

Cognos Connection initial page - My Folders

Navigating through Public Folders

Let us go back and explore the available content in the Public Folders. The content you will see is based on Cognos standard demonstration samples that are referenced multiple times throughout their official documentation, and is generally the same content used in the standard training classes.

1. Select the Public Folders tab to show its contents.

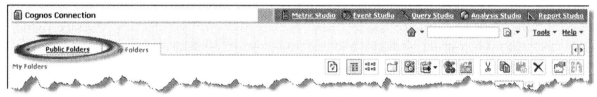

Accessing Public Folders

You will be able to see the content of the Public Folders. As you can see below, there are multiple folders of the three major types previously discussed. At least for now, we are going to focus on reports available in the Great Outdoors package (notice that this item uses the blue folder icon, which tells us this is a Package folder rather than a Standard folder).

> *If you are not using a controlled training environment, you may see additional folders listed. In some organizations, the training environment includes not only Cognos sample folders, but may include additional internal or external samples; thus, your view of the pages shown may be slightly different.*

2. Click on Great Outdoors (circled below) to access its content.

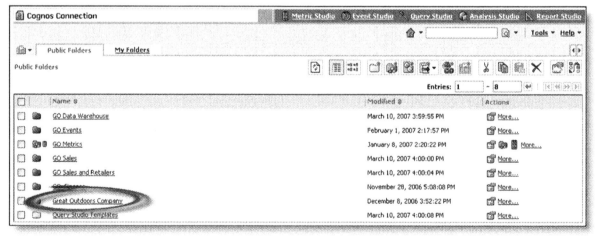

Public Folders content

By clicking the link, we can see the content of the Great Outdoors Company folder. Note that at the top of the page, just below the Public Folders tab, our location in the hierarchy of folders is shown. Remember, this is better known as the **navigation path**.

As you can see, there are three Standard folders available in this Package. The reports we will use for our tutorial are located in the Report Studio Report Samples folder.

3. Click on Report Studio Report Samples (circled below) to access its content.

Great Outdoors content

Now we can see the content of the Report Studio Report Samples folder, where many reports are listed. The default view in Cognos Connection is called the **List View,** which shows an alphabetical list of the available objects. There is another view called the **Details View** that shows additional information about the available objects, which is often useful when there is a long list of reports. Let us switch to the Details View.

4. Click on the Details View icon (second icon circled below) to access detailed information.

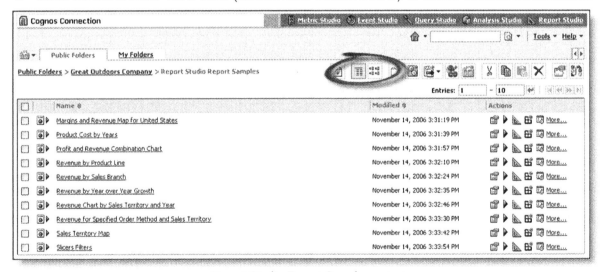

Report Studio Report Samples content

Details View – will display items in a table format with additional information available, such as descriptions.

The page now shows the objects with their corresponding detailed descriptions.

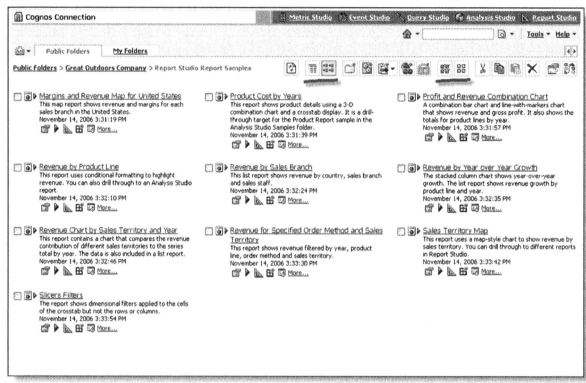

Cognos Connection displayed with Details View

Notice that when using the Details View, you have two additional icons available to Select and Deselect All objects, which are especially useful when performing Cut & Paste operations.

Select All – Allows you to select all items in a Details View

Deselect All – Allows you to deselect all items in a Details View

5. Click the List View icon from the folder toolbar to go back to the previous format.

List view - will display items in a list format with minimum information.

Adding content to Cognos Connection

There are several types of objects that can be added to Cognos Connection by Consumers. Those objects can customize the organization in Cognos Connection and add additional functionality.

Creating Folders

Up until now, we have navigated through pre-defined folders. However, let us say that we want to create a new folder to store the multiple samples we will be creating during this tutorial.

1. Click on the New Folder icon (circled below) to create a new Standard Folder. There are other options for creating the other types of folders (Packages and Metric Packages), but they are more advanced options not available for Consumers; these will be discussed in subsequent books.

Creating a new Standard Folder

New Folder – Used to create new Standard Folder.

The New Folder Wizard will appear and ask you to supply the required information needed to create the new folder.

2. By merely specifying a Name (1) and Location (2), in this case by clicking Select My Folders, we are able to create a new folder. Other information that can be added includes a detailed Description that will display when the navigator is on Details View, and a Screen tip that will pop up on the page whenever the user positions the mouse over that folder.

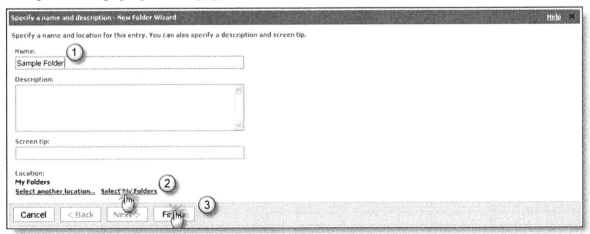

The New Folder Wizard initial page

After clicking "Finish" (3), the new folder is created in the specified folder; in this case, in My Folders.

3. Select the My Folders tab to see our new folder (circled below).

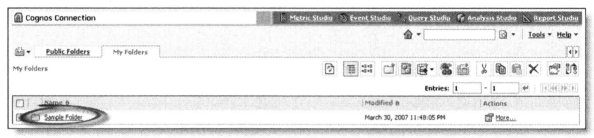

New Sample Folder created on My Folders

As mentioned earlier, a folder is a container used to organize content, much like a manila folder, which helps you organize your paper documents.

4. Click on Sample Folder to see its contents.

Inside the new Sample Folder

Of course, this new folder, although available, is empty. So let us put some content in it.

Copy the "Revenue by Product Line" report into the newly created folder from the Public Folders area. Find this report by navigating through the tabs and folders on your own, and when you find it, select it by placing a check box just beside its name. (If you are not sure about the navigation, go back and review Chapter 2: Cognos 8 BI Quick Tour.)

Once you have found the report and selected it, use the built-in functionality of Copy and Paste to make a copy of the report in the new folder you just created.

5. Select the report (1), press the Copy icon (2) and go back to My Folders > Sample Folder
    (3) to paste it. (When you get to My Folders, do not forget to navigate into Sample Folder
    before pasting.)

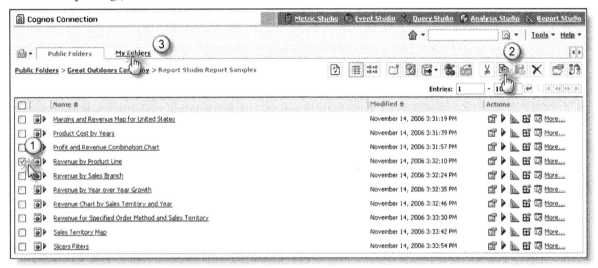

Copying a BI object into another folder

 Copy – used to copy selected objects (items with a checkmark). You can
select one or more objects to copy at the same time.

In My Folders > Sample Folder, the Paste icon is now enabled.

6. Click the Paste icon (1) to add the report to this folder.

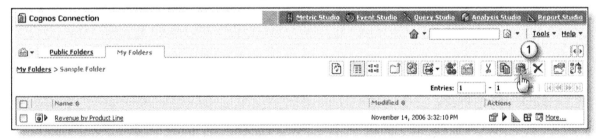

Pasting a BI object into a folder

 Paste – Used to copy the content stored in the internal clipboard to a new
location.

 Disabled Paste – If there is no content in the internal clipboard, the Paste
option will appear disabled.

---

*You may notice that the Paste icon was disabled before you pressed the Copy icon. The Paste
functionality is enabled only when there is content in the internal clipboard available for pasting.*

As you can see, a copy of the report is now available in the Sample Folder. Other options allow for moving and deleting Cognos Connection contents. They follow the same standard process as Copy.

✂ **Cut** – Used in conjunction with the Paste icon to move (not copy) the content or report stored in the internal clipboard to a new location.

✗ **Delete** – Used to permanently delete content from Cognos Connection. This option will always give you the option to confirm before deleting the object.

Creating URL links

Reports are not the only objects you can store in My Folders. You can also store links to web pages.

1. Click on the New URL icon (circled below) to create a new URL link. By creating URL links, you can simplify how users can access content on internal and external web sites.

URL stands for Uniform Resource Locator and is the standard for web addresses. The most common are those starting with "http://" as in http://www.cognos.com to connect to Cognos Corporate web site

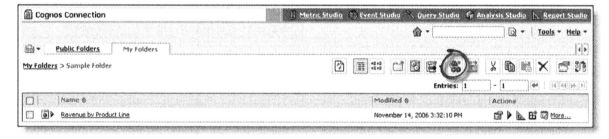

Creating a new URL

 New URL – Used to create new URL links to web sites.

The New URL Wizard will appear and ask you the required information to create the new URL.

2. By specifying a Name (1), Screen tip (2), URL (3) and folder Location (4), we are able to create a new URL link in our folder list. (Click Finish when ready.)

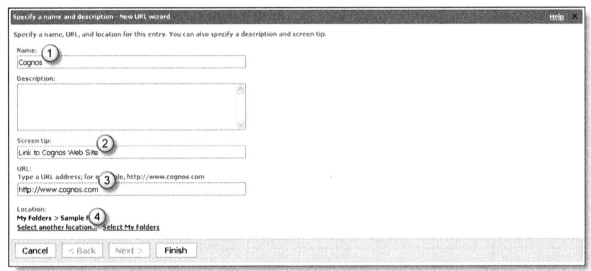

The URL Wizard initial page

The new URL has been created and stored in the specified folder. You can see the difference between the URL and Report icons.

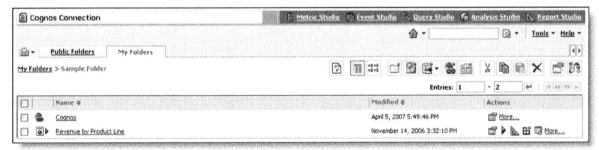

Content in the Sample Folder

We now have two objects in our new Sample Folder.

Sorting Content

As you begin to store more and more objects in a folder, you may want to organize the objects, such as displaying all the URLs together, displaying the reports in the list before the URLs, or sorting objects by the date modified. By default, items are displayed alphabetically in the folders.

To change the order in which the objects are presented, you can click on the icons beside the headers in the Cognos Connection List View. (See circled items in the image below.)

Changing list sorting criteria

By selecting the icon beside the Name header, you will sort the objects in alphabetical order. By selecting the Modified header, you will be able to sort chronologically. You can also sort in either ascending or descending order.

- ⇕   No Sort – Do not sort for that column
- ▲   Sort Ascending – Sort by that column ascending
- ▼   Sort Descending – Sort by that column descending

Although the above options allow you to sort dynamically on an "as needed" basis, they are somewhat limited.

Custom Sorting

You can also create your own customized sorting by selecting the Custom Order option.

1. Click on the Custom Order icon (circled below) to define your customized sorting criteria.

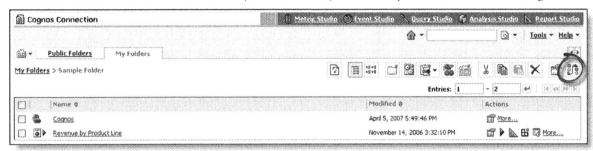

Custom Order option

The **Order folders and entries** page will appear and let you specify the order criteria for both folders and entries in the container. Note that at the top of the page, after the page title, it specifies that you are currently in the "Sample Folder". This lets you know you are customizing the sort criteria for the information contained within that folder.

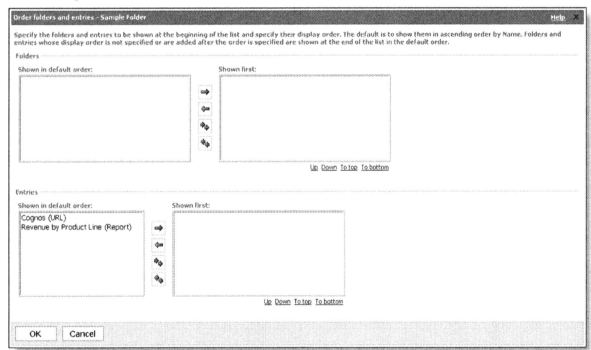

Order folders and entries page

2. Select the Revenue by Product Line report from the "Shown in default order" list (1) and add it to the "Shown first" box by clicking the right-pointing arrow (2) to establish the desired order. Do the same for the Cognos URL.

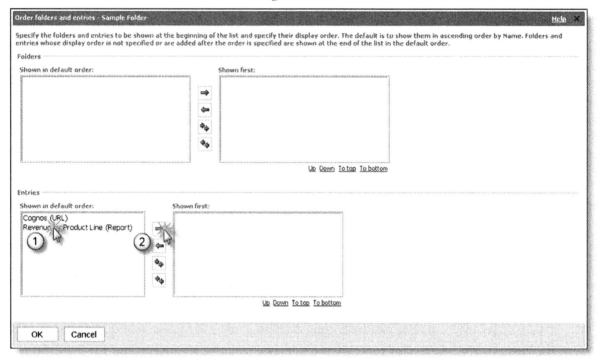

Ordering entries

By moving these items from the left-hand list to the right-hand list and using the other ordering options (Up, Down, To Top and To Bottom arrows), you can establish a customized order of objects in your list.

Remember that this is a non-dynamic way to sort the entries, i.e. these custom options will be used every time you use Cognos Connection, so you will have to enter this page again if you add additional entries and want to modify their order, or if you want to change the custom options you previously created.

---

3. Click OK to apply the custom order configuration.

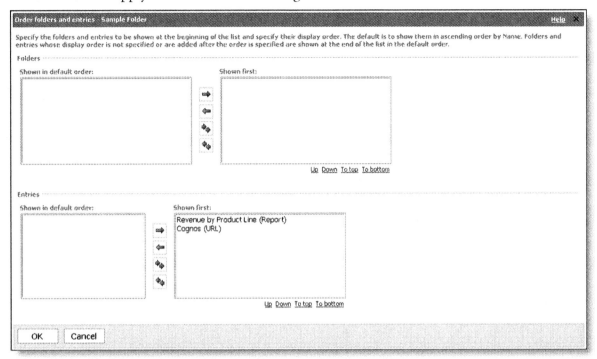

Customized order

As you can see, the entries in the folder are now sorted based on our custom definition.

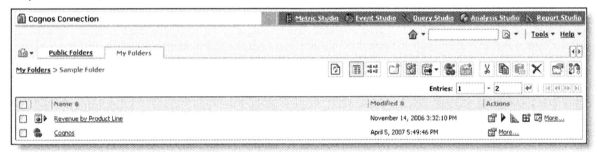

List with customized order

Let's practice! Try to delete the Cognos URL from My Folders!

Modifying properties

Besides sorting, there are other folder properties that can be modified.

1. Click on the Set properties icon (circled below) to access the folder's properties.

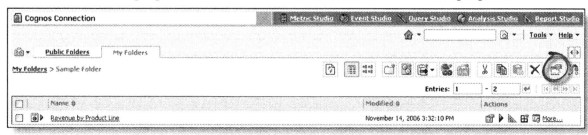

Set Properties option

 Set properties – Allows for maintenance of internal object properties, such as general information, permissions and other object-specific properties.

Most of the time, the Set properties page will display General information, which includes Name, Description, Screen tip, Owner, Location and other general information.

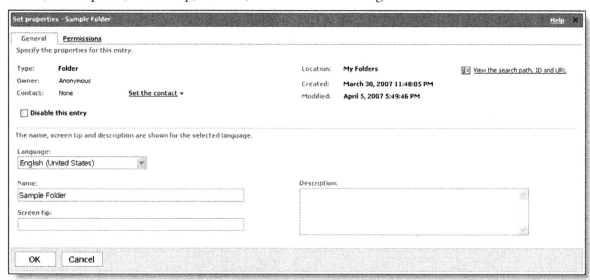

Set properties – General information

For multilingual deployments, you will need to set properties in each language by first choosing from the Language list, specifying your additional language and then entering the Name, Description and Screen tip. Once Consumers change their language preferences, they will see those values. Do this for each language deployed.

A very interesting option called "View the search path, ID and URL" is also available on the upper right side of this page. This option provides very important information when trying to integrate Cognos Connection objects with external applications. Although as a Consumer you may not be involved in this type of integration, it's good to understand the options that appear on the Cognos pages; thus, let us take a moment to explain further.

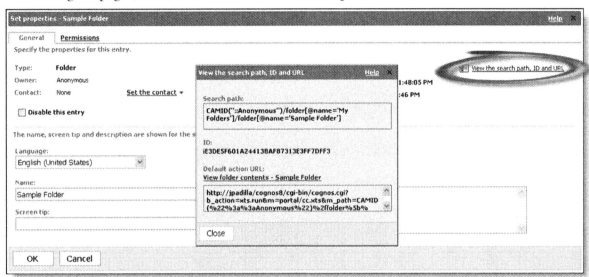

View the search path, ID and URL option

The first two options are quite technical for Consumers. *Search path* is used for advanced internal options (e.g., complex filters) and during integration using the Software Development Kit (SDK) from external applications, and *ID* is the Unique Identifier of the object in Cognos Connection. However, the last one, *Default action URL*, is very important and can be quite useful. It shows the full URL to a specific object in Cognos 8 BI. By copying and pasting it into a web browser, you will automatically be connected directly to the object you are looking for. For example, if you are creating a web page and want to display a specific Cognos report, by specifying that URL you can have direct access to it (of course, taking into account security permissions).

In addition to General Properties, you can also see information on the Permissions Properties by clicking the other tab on the Set Properties page (see below). "Permissions" include who has which access to what BI object in Cognos. Permissions in Cognos are *inherited*, which means that objects in a folder inherit the permissions of the folder, which inherits permissions from any parent folders, and so on.

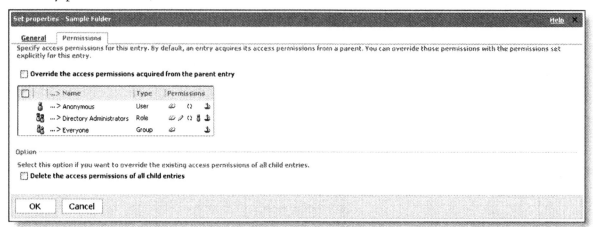

Set Properties – Permissions

For certain objects, there will be more tabs in the Set properties page. For objects such as queries, analyses, reports and so on, an additional middle tab which contains specific information regarding the object will appear. For example, in a report, the middle tab shows properties such as default action, default format, parameters, and others.

Running Reports

In this chapter, we covered the organization and creation of multiple objects and folders; however, let us say that we are interested in actually running and viewing a report. Selecting a report will render it in the Cognos 8 BI standard report viewer: Cognos Viewer. This is the topic of our next chapter.

5

Chapter 5: Cognos Viewer

The Cognos Viewer is the Cognos 8 BI standard report viewer utility. It allows a standardized look and feel among the multiple components of the suite, with standard functions for switching report formats, saving and emailing reports, and drilling and navigating through related reports.

Viewing Reports

When you select a report in Cognos Connection, it will automatically display in Cognos Viewer, the standard report viewer for Cognos 8 BI. In some cases, the report will actually start to execute, and you will see a report-running page and may have to wait for it to finish. In other cases, the report will display immediately meaning that it was previously run and the output was stored for later viewing.

Let us see how this actually works.

1. Click on "Revenue by Product Line" to execute the report. (By now, you should be comfortable navigating through folders to locate reports; if not, go back to the earlier chapters for a quick review.)

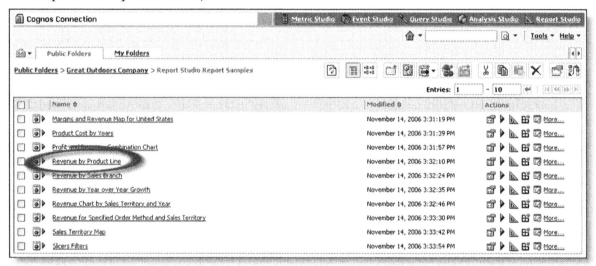

Executing a report

This will activate the report. If the report output is not already available, the report will start running, and the output will be shown. Notice that you can select the option of not waiting for the report by specifying a delivery method (discussed later on); this frees you to do other work while your report is running behind-the-scenes.

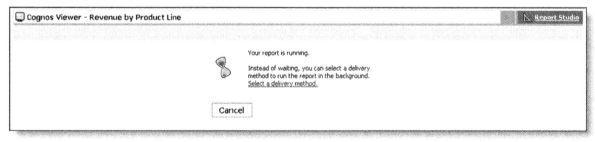

The report being executed

When the report is ready, the output of the report will be shown in Cognos Viewer.

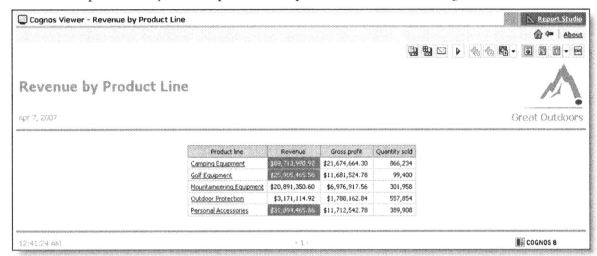

Output of the report

In the top left corner, we see the title "Cognos Viewer" along with the selected report's title. Most of the functionality of Cognos Viewer is available using its own standard toolbar at the top right. Although the toolbar is dynamic and options may vary based on the type of report and its status, this is the most common configuration.

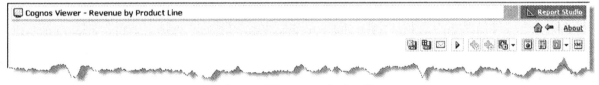

Cognos Viewer standard toolbar

The Cognos Viewer toolbar has multiple functions that we will discuss shortly.

At the top right-most corner, some users may see a link to Report Studio or some of the other studios. This functionality is reserved for higher levels of licensing; for example, to access the Report Studio link you will need Professional Author licensing or higher. As we are not using security, you are seeing the link for reference only.

Saving a report

The first option in the Cognos Viewer standard toolbar is Saving a report. Instead of generating a report and waiting around for it to be ready, we can generate it and store the output at the Cognos Connection so we can review it later.

1. To save the current output in the Cognos Viewer, click on the "Save Report" icon (circled below).

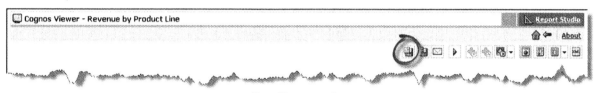

Save Report option

Save Report – will save the currently displayed report output to Cognos Connection as the default output

Your report output will be saved to Cognos Connection. Although the system does not give you any visual confirmation that the report was saved, as soon as you return to Cognos Connection you will see the report listed there.

2. Press the Return icon (circled below) to go back to Cognos Connection.

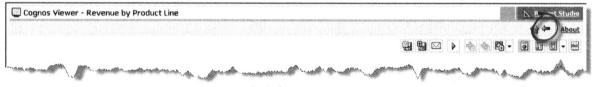

Going back from Cognos Viewer

Return – will take you to the previous Cognos Connection page.

The Return icon will take you to the exact page in Cognos Connection where you were previously located. It is different from the Home option, which will always take you to your designated Home Page, which may not have been your most recent page.

Once we return to Cognos Connection, there are some indicators (circled below) next to your report title that show the report has been generated and saved.

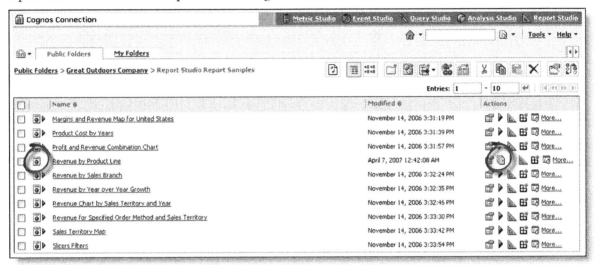

Indicators of a saved report output

The first indication that a report has been generated and saved is that the blue arrow next to the report name is missing; this means that the report will *not* be executed again when you click on that report title, but the saved output from the previous report execution will be presented. Additionally, a new icon appears under the report actions column showing that there are saved report outputs available to you.

3. Click on the report "Revenue by Product Line" to view the recently executed report using Cognos Viewer.

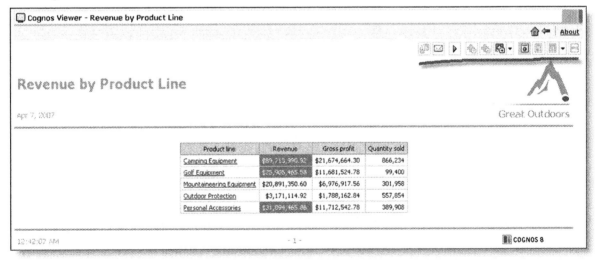

Showing the saved report

The saved report will appear instantly. Notice that the toolbar is a little different in that some icons are missing and others are disabled. This is because you are viewing a saved report from a previous report execution, so the available functionality is limited.

4. Press the Run Report icon (circled below) to execute the report again dynamically (vs. viewing the saved report).

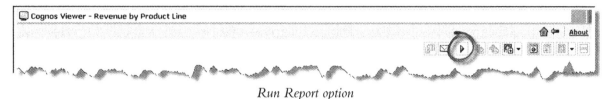

Run Report option

> ▷   **Run Report** – will execute the report with standard options.

By running the report dynamically, the default icons return.

Saving as Report View

The second option in the Cognos Viewer standard toolbar is Save as Report View. A Report View is a link to a report that we can customize to display the same report output, but with different parameters and/or formats.

1. Click on the Save as Report View icon (circled below) to create a new report view.

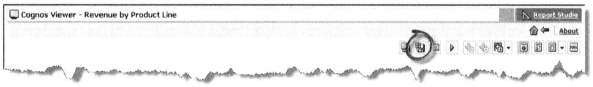

Save as Report View option

> ▦   **Save as Report View** – will create a report view based on the currently displayed report.

2. Enter the name of the new report view. Also select the "Select another location ..." option, located just above the OK/Cancel buttons, before saving it. This is important because the current report is located in the Public Folders tab, and since security will probably prevent us from saving new objects in Public Folders, we need to specify a new location to save our report view.

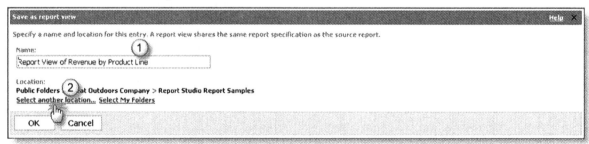

Save as report view page

3. We will need to navigate through the available folders to choose where to save the new Report View. By default, the current folder is displayed as shown below.

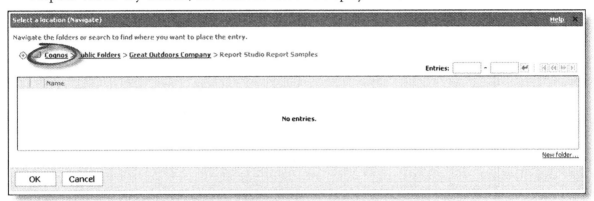

Select a location navigation page

4. When we click on Cognos in the current navigation path, we are taken back to the highest level in the folder structure. There we can choose between Public and My Folders.

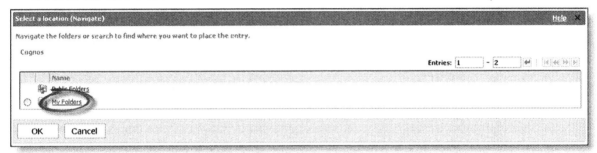

Choosing between Public and My Folders

Because we want to keep our tutorial data nicely organized, let us use our Sample Folder to store any new objects.

5. Click on My Folders label and select the Sample Folder by clicking the circle to the left of "Sample Folder", which "fills in" the circle. Press OK to save your selection.

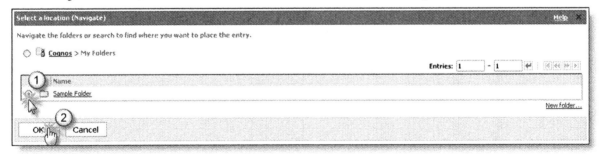

Choose the Sample Folder in My Folders

By selecting the Sample Folder, we have all the information needed to store the new Report View.

6. Click OK to complete the operation and create the new Report View in the location My
    Folders > Sample Folder.

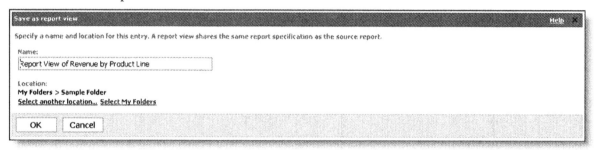

Create the new report view

By returning to Cognos Connection, we are able to see the new Report View in our list of
entries. In the upcoming chapters on Working with BI Objects and Scheduling BI Objects, we
will explore the powerful functionality of using Report Views.

Emailing Reports

The third option allows you to send a report by email to other Consumers, others in your
organization who do not use Cognos, and even to people outside your organization directly
from Cognos Viewer.

1. Click on the Email Report icon (circled below) to specify the email options for the report.

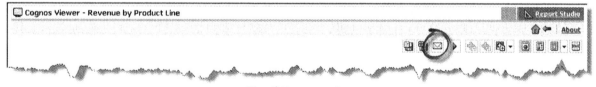

Email Report option

✉ **Email Report** – will email the currently displayed report to a list of emails to
   be specified.

2. Enter the email information. You can type email addresses in the To: and Cc: fields, or
    choose from the "Select the recipients …" to select users, roles, groups and contacts from a
    directory of internal Cognos users. Enter the subject and body of the email, and specify if
    you want to include the actual report, a link to it in Cognos Connection, or both.

> *The Select the recipients option (see below) will navigate to the security namespaces for users, roles
> and groups to share information; this topic will be discussed further in the Security chapter at the
> end of the guide.*

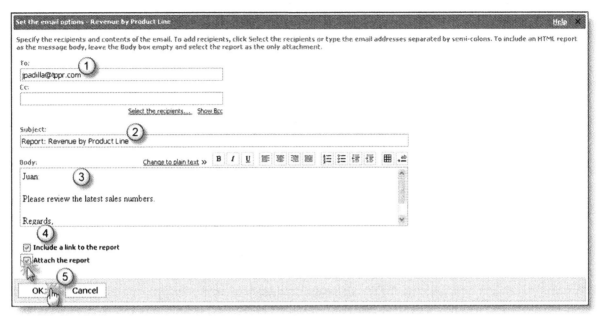

Set the email options page

As the above page shows, you can control some formatting of the body of the email using the options provided, such as adding bold or italicized text, adding bulleted lists, and changing the justification of the text in the message.

After you press OK, the email will be sent by the server.

Cognos 8 BI is a server-based tool that you can access through a web browser; thus, in order to send emails from Cognos 8 BI, the server has to be configured accordingly.

Changing report output formats

The last four options from the Cognos Viewer standard toolbar deal with report formats. Directly from Cognos Viewer, the Consumer can switch between several available formats for the report output. Those formats include HTML, PDF, MS Excel 2000 and 2002, Comma Delimited (CSV) and XML.

Viewing the report in PDF format

Adobe Acrobat PDF is one of the most widely used and standardized document formats. PDF captures a document in its original format, whether it started out as a Word or Excel file, a WordPerfect document, an image file, or any number of other file types, including a Cognos report. It then creates a "snapshot" of the original in a common format (PDF) so that users can share the document even if they don't have the same software that originally created it. With Cognos, this is a great feature as it enables you to share Cognos reports with people who may not have access to Cognos itself!

The free Adobe Acrobat Reader tool lets us open PDF files to see a preview of a report on the page, which looks exactly how it will appear on paper when you print it out. This is commonly referred to as WYSIWYG (pronounced "wizzy-wig"), which stands for What You See Is What You Get. You can think of a PDF report as the equivalent of "electronic paper"—it can't be changed without changing the original document or report, ensuring that if you send someone a Cognos report in PDF, no one can alter the data in that report.

1. Click on the View in PDF Format icon (circled below) to change the report format to PDF.

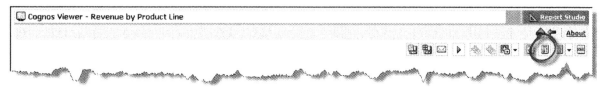

View in PDF Format option

    View in PDF Format – converts the currently displayed report to Adobe Acrobat PDF format.

Now that we are viewing the report as a PDF file (see next image), let us see what happens if we *save* the report as a PDF.

2. Click on Save the Report to save it to Cognos Connection in PDF format.

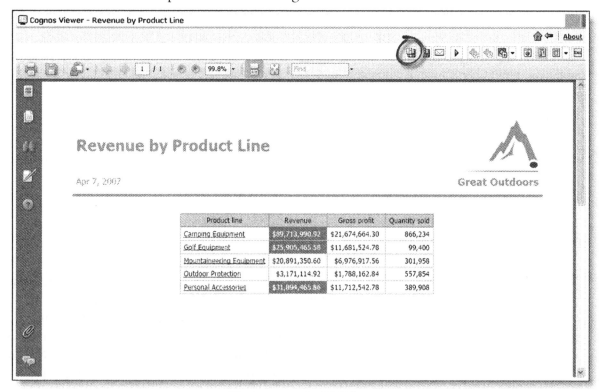

Viewing report in PDF format

The report has been saved to Cognos Connection in its current format. Let us go back to Cognos Connection to see the list of reports again.

3. Click on the Return icon to go back to Cognos Connection. This will take you back to the Cognos Connection listing.

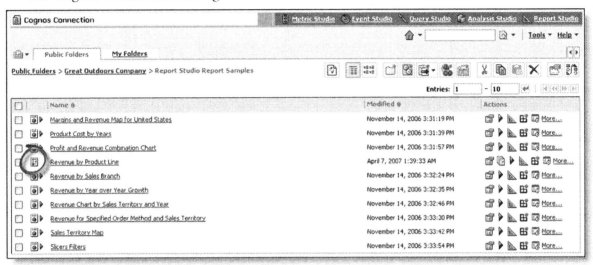

List of reports in Cognos Connection

As you can see, the list of reports in Cognos Connection now shows that the Revenue by Product Line is saved, and the icon has changed to the PDF format icon; when you click on the report, it will display in the Cognos Viewer as a PDF document. Try it! As previously stated, the functionality of the saved report is limited, so click on Run the Report to enable the format conversion icons.

Viewing the report in Microsoft Excel format

It is common for users to want to re-enter information from reports into MS Excel, so Cognos 8 BI facilitates the process by automatically transferring information from Cognos Viewer into MS Excel files.

4. Click on the View in MS Excel 2000 Single Sheet Format icon (circled below) to transfer the report data into MS Excel files.

View in MS Excel 2000 Single Sheet Format option

View in MS Excel 2000 Single Sheet Format – generates an equivalent report in MS Excel 2000 Single Sheet Format and sends it to MS Internet Explorer for viewing with the default MS Excel option.

Cognos Viewer will generate the report in MS Excel 2000 Single Sheet format and will send it to MS Internet Explorer for processing.

By default, MS Internet Explorer will ask you what you want to do with the report. You may have this option already set to open the file automatically and, therefore, you may not get this page.

MS Internet Explorer confirmation page

Thus, the report should be loaded automatically into MS Excel. Notice that the formatting, including headers and footers, has also been transferred to MS Excel.

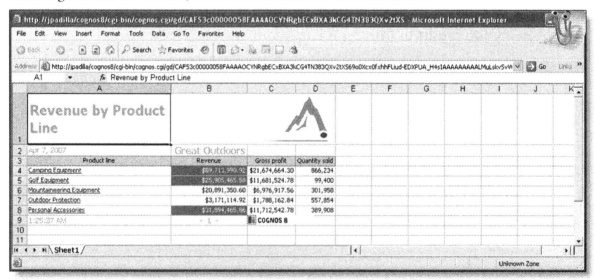

Viewing the report in MS Excel

Close the page to go back to Cognos Viewer.

There are actually several formats in which you can see the reports in MS Excel.

5. Expand the menu next to the View in MS Excel 2000 Single Sheet Format icon, as shown below, to gain access to the other available formats for MS Excel.

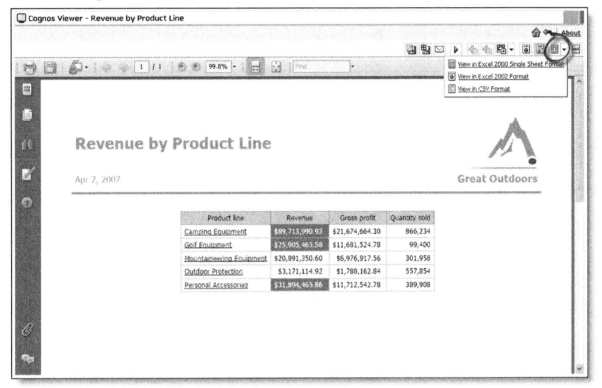

Formats available for MS Excel

⬜ **View in MS Excel 2000 Single Sheet Format** – generates an equivalent report in MS Excel 2000 Single Sheet Format and sends it to MS Internet Explorer to view with the default MS Excel option. This format will show the whole report as one worksheet.

⬜ **View in MS Excel 2002 Format** – generates an equivalent report in MS Excel 2002 and sends it to MS Internet Explorer to view with the default MS Excel option. This format will show each page as an individual worksheet.

⬜ **View in CSV Format** – generates an equivalent report in CSV format (comma delimited) and sends it to MS Internet Explorer to view with the default MS Excel option. This option will only send data and will not show any layout format.

6. Select the View in CSV format to show only the report data.

View report in MS Excel as CSV

Close the page to go back to Cognos Viewer.

Viewing the report in XML or HTML format

XML and HTML formats are used to transfer information between certain XML-friendly applications in a format that can be easily automated or interpreted by those applications (such as web-based applications). Both XML and HTML are similar in that they enclose data into a set of "tags" that will define the starting and ending points of the data formatting.

7. Click on the View in XML Format icon to change the report format to XML.

View in XML Format option

> **View in XML Format** – converts the currently displayed report to XML format.

This will show the report in XML format.

```
<?xml version="1.0" encoding="utf-8" ?>
- <dataset xmlns="http://developer.cognos.com/schemas/xmldata/1/" xmlns:xs="http://www.w3.org/2001/XMLSchema-
    instance">
- <!--
     <dataset
          xmlns="http://developer.cognos.com/schemas/xmldata/1/"
          xmlns:xs="http://www.w3.org/2001/XMLSchema-instance"
          xs:schemaLocation="http://developer.cognos.com/schemas/xmldata/1/ xmldata.xsd"
     >
   -->
- <metadata>
     <item name="Product line" type="xs:string" length="-1" />
     <item name="Revenue" type="xs:double" precision="2" />
     <item name="Gross profit" type="xs:double" precision="2" />
     <item name="Quantity sold" type="xs:double" precision="2" />
   </metadata>
- <data>
   - <row>
       <value>Camping Equipment</value>
       <value currency="USD">89713990.92</value>
       <value currency="USD">21674664.3</value>
       <value>866234</value>
     </row>
   - <row>
       <value>Golf Equipment</value>
       <value currency="USD">25905465.58</value>
       <value currency="USD">11681524.78</value>
       <value>99400</value>
     </row>
   - <row>
       <value>Mountaineering Equipment</value>
```

Viewing report in XML format

8. Click on the View in HTML Format to change it to the most standard format in Cognos
    Connection.

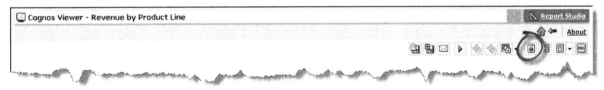

View in HTML Format option

View in HTML Format – automatically convert the currently displayed
report to HTML format.

Cognos Connection should now display the report in HTML format.

Navigating through Reports

Cognos 8 BI allows you to navigate inside a report or from one report to another, seamlessly exchanging context information so the data in the called report is related to the calling one.

Drilling Through

The process of navigating from one report to another is called **Drill Through**. Drilling Through is quite simple: merely click on the available hyperlinks to access other related reports.

1. In the Revenue by Product Line report, click on the hyperlink called Camping Equipment.

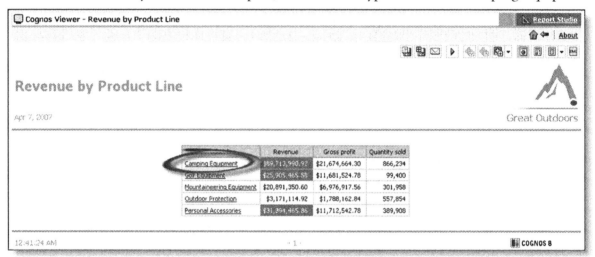

Click on hyperlink to Drill Through another report

This will execute the Drill Through report passing Camping Equipment as a filter. The resulting report will show Revenue by Years and Order Methods analyzed by Sales Territory for Camping Equipment only. At the top of the report, you will see an icon that shows we have filtered the information for Camping Equipment.

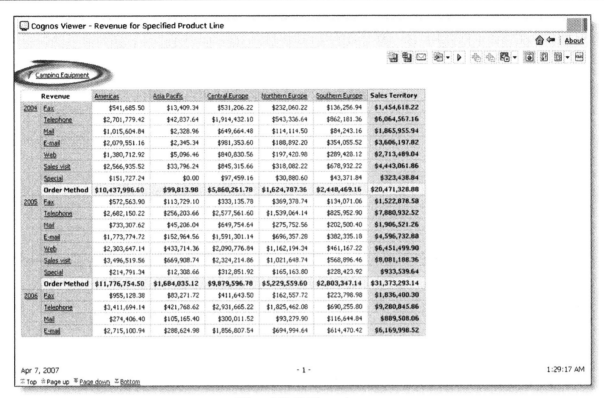

Filtered Drill Through report

Using this report, we will explore some additional interesting functionalities.

Drilling through is very useful. A Power User can define standard detail reports for main business entities, such as Customer, Employee, Product and Vendor, among others. Then from any report, the user can set up Drill Through to get detailed information quickly and easily by calling those standard reports.

Drilling Down

The process of navigating internally within a report is called **Drill Down**. Drilling Down is quite simple; just click on the available hyperlinks to navigate, or drill down, into deeper levels of detail.

Let us try it using the Camping Equipment drill-through we just executed.

2. Click the year 2004 in the report.

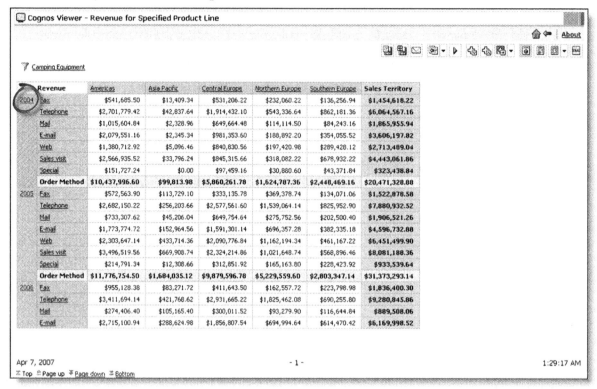

Available options in field

This is the concept of Drill Down. Drill Down allows you to navigate down into levels of a dimension to get information that is more granular. In our example, the year is a dimension with multiple levels beneath it; those levels are Year, Quarter and Month, and you can navigate (drill down and drill up) through those levels.

Dimensions and levels must be preconfigured by developers or administrators, and are then available for everyone with adequate permissions.

Alternatively, you can use the right mouse button over the year 2004 in the report. A menu with several options will appear. Select Drill Down.

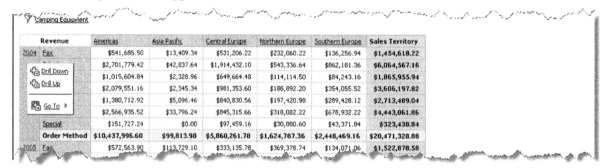

In our example, we chose to view Quarterly information within the year 2004; thus, instead of the years, we now see the 2004 quarters.

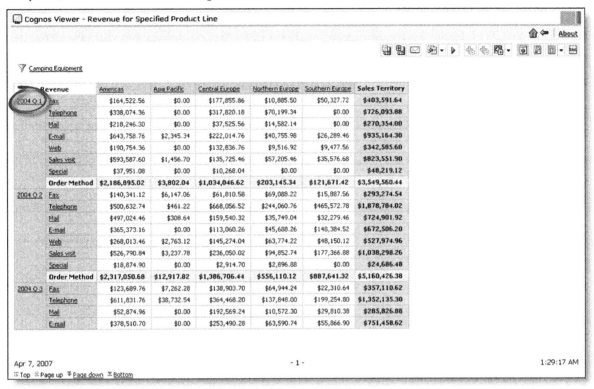

Drilling down from Year to Quarter

3. Go back to the Year by choosing Drill Up from the right mouse-button menu (click with your right mouse button over the Quarter).

Drilling Through standard reports

Drill Throughs are usually defined in reports by specifying the target report and defining the parameters to pass between them. This is a process that a Power User, not a Consumer or a Developer, usually performs when developing reports. These Drill Throughs are easily identified because a hyperlink is available as a visual aid to let you know that something can be clicked for more information.

On the other side, there are some standard Drill Through options for all reports that are based on a specific package. These Drill Throughs are not reflected by a hyperlink, but have to be accessed by other available options in Cognos Viewer. To access these reports, you have to use the Go To option in the Cognos Viewer toolbar.

4. Click on the Go To option from the Cognos Viewer toolbar.

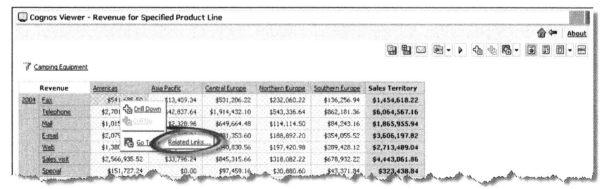

Go To option

![Go To icon] **Go To** – Drill Through to other available reports in the package.

Another way to do this is the "context-sensitive option". Using your right mouse button, click over fields in the report to show the Go To option and the Related Links below it. Let us try to use the context-sensitive option in Cognos Viewer.

5. Do you see the cell under the Americas column and the 2004 Fax row? Click the right mouse button in that cell, and select Related Links… under Go To.

Right mouse button Go To option

A list of the available links will appear in a new window.

6. Click on Revenue for Specified Order Method and Sales Territory to access that report.

Available links for Drill Through

When you select a link, the context (Fax and Americas) in the first report where you selected the option is passed to the second report.

As you can see, the report is filtered by Fax and Americas.

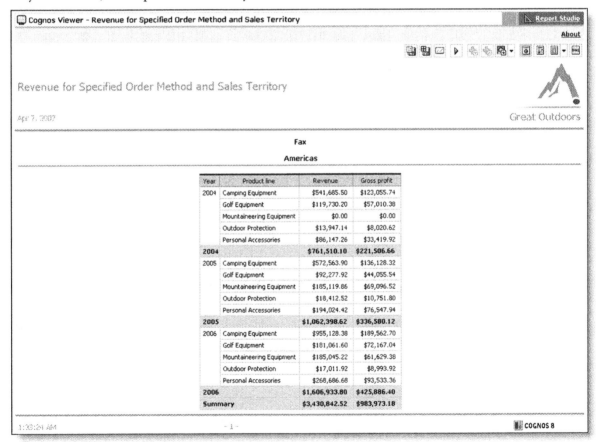

Standard drill through report

Close the report window to go back to Cognos Connection.

Return to Previous Report

Once you have finished with the Drill Through report and want to return to the original, there is a Return To Previous Report option that will bring you back.

Do not use the Return or Home options because they take you to Cognos Connection, and if you are in a Drill Through report, you probably would prefer to stay in Cognos Viewer in your original report.

---

7. Click on Return to Previous Report to go back to the original.

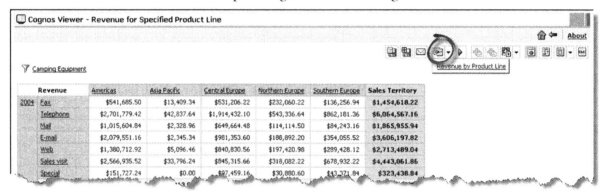

Return to Previous Report option

Return to Previous Report – takes you to the original calling report in Cognos Viewer.

Parameters

Reports can be developed so they will ask for user input to dynamically filter data and customize the report layout. This is called **passing parameters to a report**. In Cognos 8 BI, when a report that requires parameters is executed, it will automatically display a prompt requesting the user input. The prompt is the actual user interface for the user to pass parameters to a report.

If you add Cognos reports to a web page, you can customize the report URL link shown previously in the properties of the report to include the parameters and desired values so the report can execute without additionally prompting for values.

Cognos 8 BI has an extensive variety of prompt options. We are going to focus on a single standard option to show the available functionality and its common use. In the appendix, we include screenshots of sample reports that use multiple prompt types, such as text fields, lists and calendars, among others.

1. Choose the Revenue by Sales Branch report that is available in the same folder as the Revenue by Product Line report used before. (By now, you should be comfortable navigating through folders to locate reports; if not, go back to the earlier chapters for a quick review.)

Specifying parameters

When you click on the report, a parameter page that asks for which country you want to run the report is shown. As you can see, the prompt is presented as a list. That list can be configured by the Power User to have predefined values or to read data directly from the source, so it is dynamically generated and updated. In this case, it shows names of countries from which to choose. In other cases, such as when asking for a date, Cognos 8 BI can show you a calendar, or if you are asking for multiple values, display a multi-line list instead of a drop-down list.

Two icons next to this prompt are quite important.

* **Indicates a required field** – means that a value must be provided for the prompt, or the options to continue in the bottom will not be enabled.

* **Points to missing information** – means that the prompt does not have a value assigned to it. If the prompt is not required, this will not be a problem and you can continue to run the report without issues.

By selecting a value and complying with the prompt requirements, the options to continue should be activated.

2. Choose one of the countries: United States.

Choosing a value

As you can see, the OK button is now enabled, which allows you to execute the report.

The prompt functionality is quite powerful and very simple for Power Users to create and Consumers to use. In the sample reports in the appendix, you will be able to see other advanced prompt types available. There is even one report that uses cascade prompts, which means that prompts can depend on other prompts; for example, a City prompt can be restricted by a Country prompt.

Other options for working with BI Objects

Objects such as reports have many other available options, properties and actions that we can set up in Cognos Connection. We will explore those in detail in the next chapter.

6

Chapter 6: Working with BI Objects

Every BI Object has standard options available in Cognos Connection that define its behavior. Properties can be modified to change the default behavior, manual execution can be performed to override options, and objects can be created and linked to existing objects to enhance their functionality.

Available actions

Going back to Cognos Connection, and as we navigate through the different folders (whether in the Public Folders or even in the new Sample Folder that we created), we notice that the objects stored in the folders have some available actions. These actions are designated via icons that appear just to the left of the object's Name, and in the right-hand column in the list of objects, labeled "Actions".

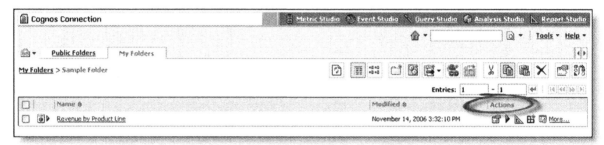

Content of the Sample Folder in My Folders with Actions shown to the right

In this chapter, we will explore the available actions, as well as how to work with each of them to set properties and options for an object.

The Default Action

Every object in Cognos Connection has a default action associated with it. For example, if you look at the content of the Sample Folder, you will notice it has an icon to the left of the object's Name (circled below). These icons describe the default action associated with that object.

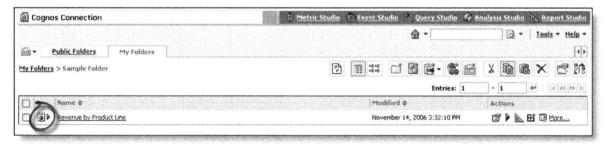

Icons that show an object's default action

As shown previously in Cognos Viewer, the first icon is the Show in HTML Format icon, while the second is the Run Report icon. This translates to "Run Report and Show in HTML Format". It is an easy way to understand and be aware of what is supposed to happen when you click on an object.

An object's default action can be configured by modifying the object's properties.

The "Set Properties" Action

Just as with the folders in My Folders, all BI objects have properties that describe them and that can be easily viewed or modified.

1. Click on the Set Properties icon (circled below) to access the report properties.

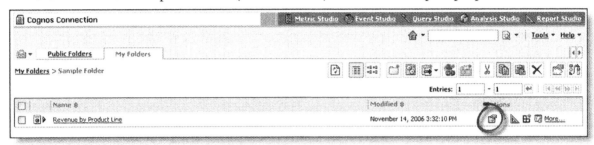

Set Properties option

> Set Properties – access to the object's properties for viewing and/or modification (with proper permissions).

This should display the Set Properties page.

Set Properties – General Properties Tab

The initial Set Properties page is usually quite standard for any BI Object. It contains general information about the object, including its name, description, screen tip, the type of object, the owner and other auditing information. On this page, you can also disable an object so it is no longer accessible by other users.

It is important to notice the "View the search path, Id and URL" option in the top right corner. This is essential if you are trying to integrate Cognos 8 with external applications, such as a web site with a direct link to a report.

In the case of a Report object, there are two options located at the bottom of the Set Properties page (see next image) that are quite useful:

• **Run history** – Defines how long the system should keep a log of historical information regarding when a report was run (executed). Run history will also list the report's status and other related information.

• **Report output versions** – Defines how many outputs of the report the system should maintain. For example, let us say that you have a report and you want to view the last three executions, perhaps to compare the data from the latest execution with the three previous ones. In order to do this, you need to set the number of versions to be saved for that report so that the system will store the prior reports.

Set Properties – Initial page

Set Properties – Middle Tab

The middle section usually contains information tightly integrated with the type of object you are looking at. For example, in this case we are looking at the properties for a Report object, so the middle tab is labeled "Report" and provides us with options to specify the default actions, report options (such as format and language), prompt values and how the report is supposed to run if performed as part of a batch. If we were setting properties for a type of object other than a Report, this middle tab might display different information relevant to that type of object.

"View most recent report" is the default option, but if a report output is not available, Cognos 8 BI will automatically execute the report and show it. This is the same functionality as setting the default to Run Report.

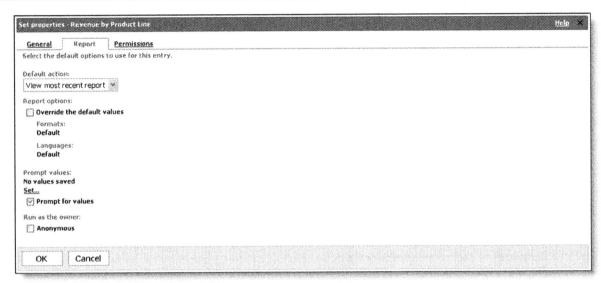

Set Properties – Middle page

Other Default actions that can be specified are:

- **Run report** – execute the report by default, even if an output is available.

- **Open with Report Studio** – open the report for modification with the tool that created it, in this case Report Studio; the option will change to Query Studio for a query, Analysis Studio for an analysis, and so on.

You can modify (override) the properties to your satisfaction.

2.   Click on Override the default values to modify some of the report properties.

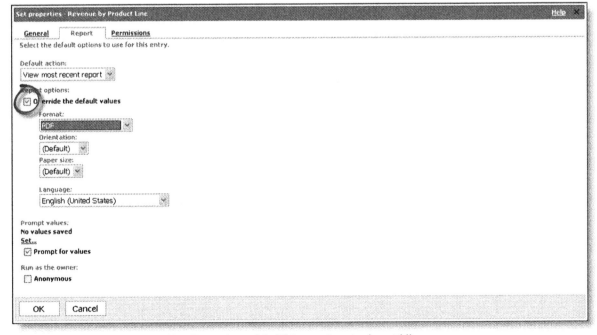

Set Properties – Modifying options in the middle page

In this case, we can modify the default format to PDF, instead of the default HTML format that was initially shown.

Set Properties – Last Page (Permissions Tab)

As the initial page, the last page is also usually quite standard for any BI Object. It has to do with permissions to access an object. The permissions are inherited from the folder where the object is located, but can easily be modified by selecting the Override option. More on that in the Security in Cognos Connection chapter.

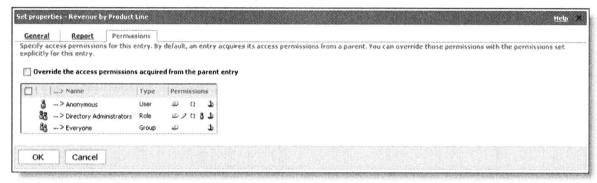

Set Properties – Last page

Run with options

If you click on an object in Cognos Connection, it will perform the default action as specified in the properties. If you want to execute the report with different options than the defaults, then you have to use the **Run with options** option.

1. Click on the Run with options icon (circled below) to execute the report with non-standard options.

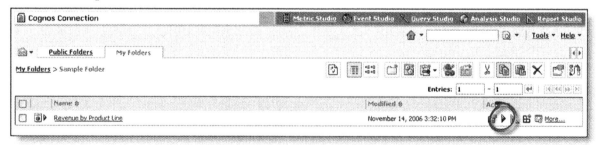

Run with options option

    ▷   **Run with options** – allows specification of non-standard options for running a report.

This will display the **Run with options** page. The initial page will let you modify basic options, such as the format, language, delivery and prompts. These are the most commonly used options, so they are presented in a simple page for fast set-up and execution. However, some advanced options are sometimes needed.

Run with options modifications are temporary configurations valid only for that specific execution. If you want these options to be permanently applied to the report execution, you have to modify the report properties.

---

2.   Click on the advanced options hyperlink for additional run options.

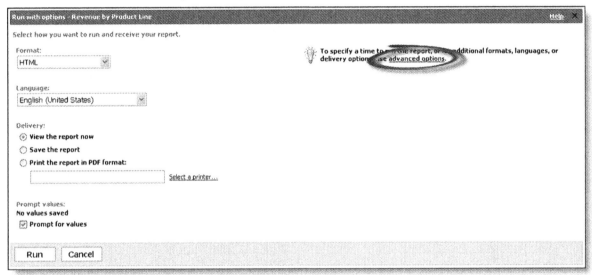

Run with options - Basic options

This will display the advanced options page.

This page will let you execute the report immediately or schedule it for later execution. It will also let you choose several output formats, languages and delivery options for the report.

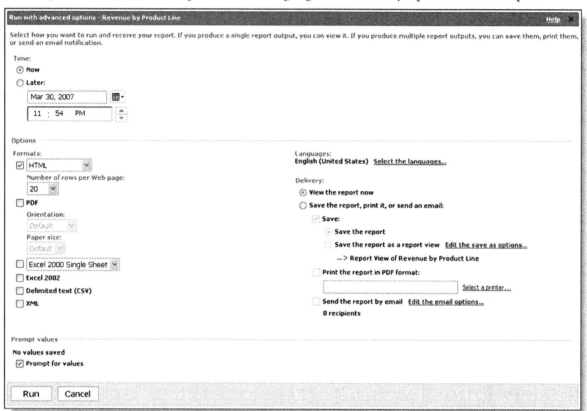

Run with options - Advanced options

Let us say that instead of executing the report in the standard "View the report as HTML" format, we want to execute the report in PDF format and save it to Cognos Connection. We can set up the options accordingly to perform that action.

3. Click on the PDF format option (1) on the left , and the Save the report option (2) on the right. Click on Run (3) when ready.

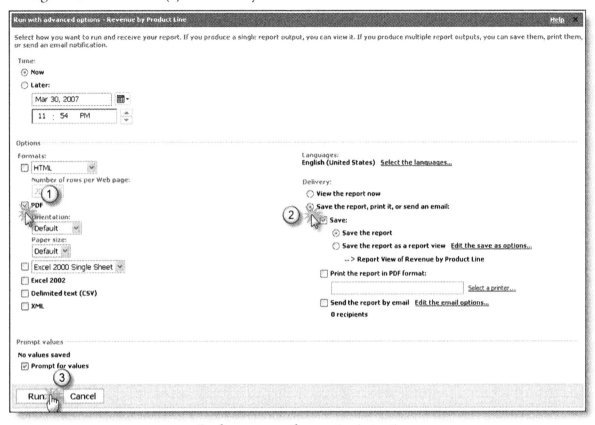

Configure my specific execution instructions

This will execute the report using your specifications. By default, a confirmation will appear. The confirmation page can be disabled in the My Preferences option in Cognos Connection.

4. Press OK to execute the report.

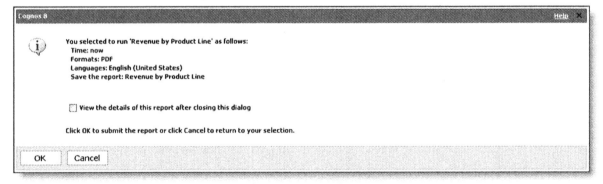

Run with options – Confirmation page

The report will be executed in the background and the output stored in Cognos Connection. After you press OK, the system will automatically bring you to the page where you selected **Run with options**.

The report will execute in the background, and will take several seconds to finish.

5. Press the Refresh icon (circled below) to see modifications in the objects.

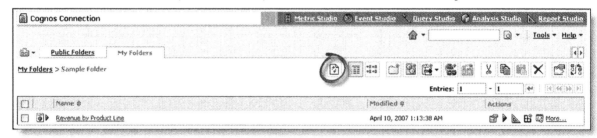

Refresh option

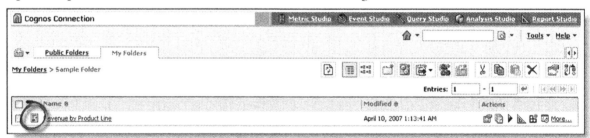 **Refresh** – will display the content of the folder with the latest specifications.

If you do not notice any change, you can press the Refresh icon every few seconds until the report is updated. Look at the Modified date until it changes.

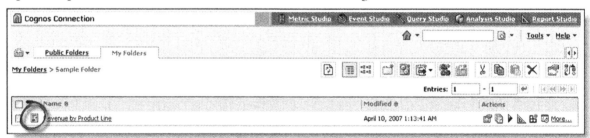

Updated Sample Folder content

Once the report is executed, look at the content in the Sample Folder where you will notice that the default action has changed and the Report Output icon is also available. This means a PDF report output is available, as specified in the Run with options preferences.

6. Press the View the output versions icon to see the report output.

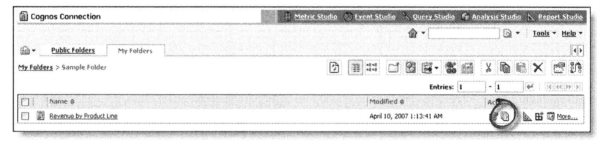

View the report output versions

You will see the report outputs, and a PDF output is now available. If you select multiple formats and/or languages, you will see multiple entries in this list of the available types of outputs for this report.

7. Press the PDF option to see the report output.

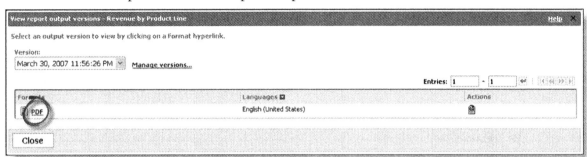

View the PDF report output

The PDF report output displays in Cognos Viewer. This is equivalent to clicking on the report name, if you chose the most recent report.

8. Press the Return option to go back to Cognos Connection.

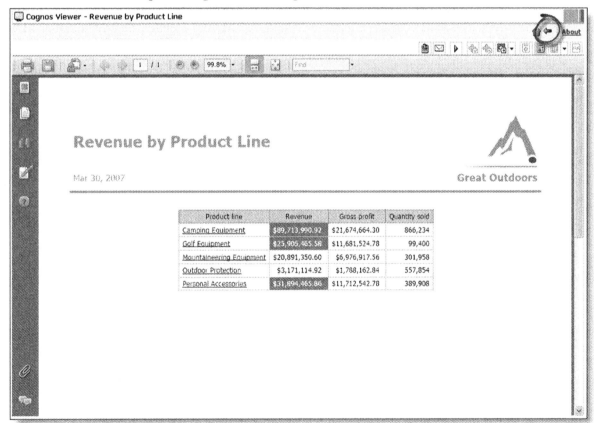

The report in PDF format

Editing Reports

To edit BI Objects, you need to have access to the specific tool used to create the object. These tools are the Studios at the top of Cognos Connection. As this guide focuses on the base Consumer role, we will not be able to edit any object. These topics will be explained in future guides, but because it is an Available option for our sample objects, we merely wanted to explain it briefly.

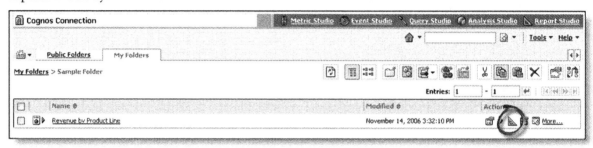

Edit an object

The icon will vary according to the Studio used to create the object.

Create a Report View

A Report View is a link to a report that can be used to specify different options or parameters than the original. For example, let us say that we have a Sales report that we want to execute for both Boston and Chicago. We can create two Report Views and specify that the first one display Sales in Boston, and in the properties, we want to set the parameter to Boston. We will also need to do the same for Chicago; thus, we will have two reports that will execute and automatically generate data related to those specific areas.

1. Click on the Create a Report View icon to create a new link to the report.

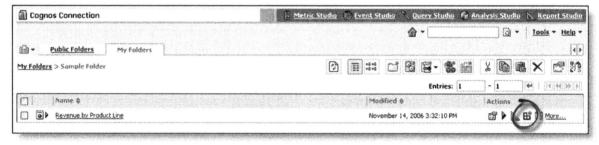

Create a Report View option

> **Create a Report View** – creates a new link to the report where options, preferences and parameters can be specified independently of the original report.

This should bring the New Report View wizard.

2. Here you can specify a name, description, screen tip and location of the new Report View. Press Finish when ready.

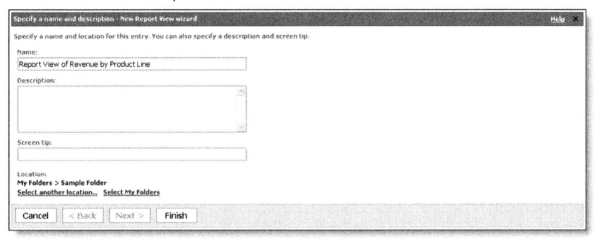

New Report View wizard

This should create a new object in Cognos Connection (see first object in list below). As you may notice, it does not have as many actions as the original report, because it is only a link to specify and store additional options, not a full-blown copy of the report.

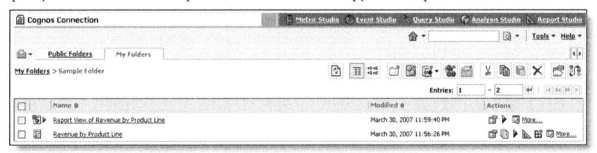

Updated listing with the original report and the report view

Scheduling a Report

From the actions, you can schedule a report to execute at specific intervals.

1. Click on the Schedule icon (circled below) to schedule a report.

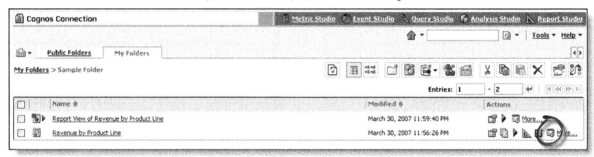

Schedule option

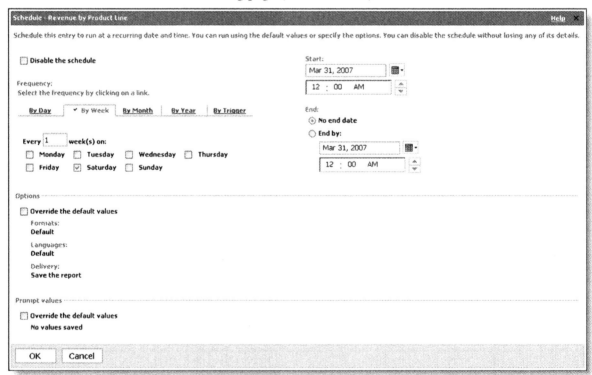

    Schedule – allows you to schedule a report for later execution. Other options, such as outputs, languages, delivery and parameters can also be specified.

This will display the Schedule page.

2. Press Cancel to exit the scheduling page (shown below) for now.

Schedule Page

We are not going to cover the scheduling options at this time, but will devote a complete chapter to scheduling reports later in the book.

Additional Actions

The most frequently used options are displayed in the list at the Tab Navigator. However, an object may have many other actions that may not be as frequently used, but which add additional features to the system.

1. Access additional actions by pressing More... (circled below).

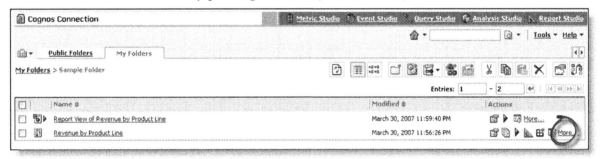

Access to additional actions using More...

A page with all the available actions for the object will appear. Notice that not only are the frequently used actions here, but also those that are used less often.

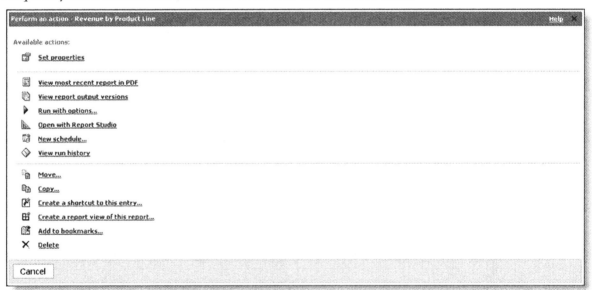

All available object actions

If you have a schedule set for the BI object, you will see two additional options for working with the schedule:

> **Modify the schedule** – to change the defined settings for the report scheduling.

> **Remove the schedule** – to remove the schedule settings so that the report is no longer executed automatically.

As the majority of the options shown in the above page have already been covered, let us focus on a few new ones.

View run history

As the report is executed, the run history will list information about the execution, including whether it was successful or not, the time of execution, the report output and any message that the report execution generated.

1. Click on the View run history icon (circled below) to view the report execution.

View run history option

◇   **View run history** – shows the report execution history.

This will display the View run history page.

2. Click on the View run history details icon (to the right, under Actions) to view the report execution details.

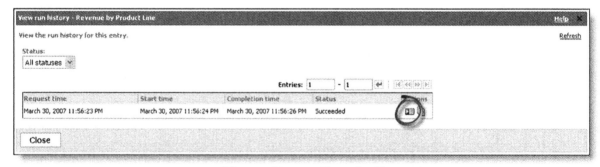

View run history – Execution list

▶▦   **View run history details** – shows the report execution information, with detailed data about times, statuses, outputs, messages, etc.

This displays the View run history details page.

3. Click on the Close button to exit the page.

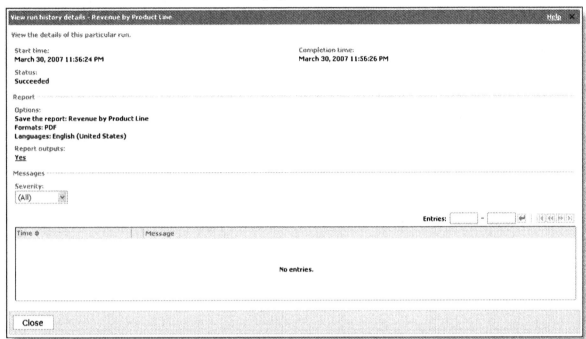

View run history – Details

Create shortcut

You can create shortcuts in Cognos Connection to have direct, fast access to reports from other folders. A shortcut differs from a report view in that the former cannot be used to specify properties and/or parameters for execution because you are actually accessing the original report directly. A shortcut is just a link to access the original report easily. The functionality of the latter can be used to specify different properties and/or parameters for execution.

1. Click on Create a shortcut for this entry to add a new link to it in any folder in Cognos Connection.

Create a shortcut option

Create a shortcut – creates a direct link to an entry that can be used to create direct access to it from different folders.

This will display the New Shortcut wizard.

2. Specify a name, description, screen tip and location of the new shortcut.   Press Finish when ready.

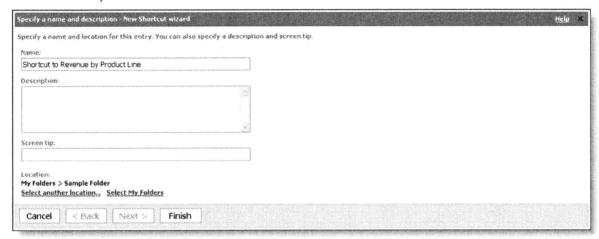

New Shortcut wizard

This should create a new Shortcut object in Cognos Connection. As you may notice, it provides the same options as the original report because it is a direct link that will let you access the original entry from multiple folders.

Updated listing with the original report and the shortcut

Be very careful when making modifications to a shortcut, because your changes will be applied to the original object as well!

Add to bookmarks

You can add a report to your browser bookmarks to access it quickly.

1. Click on Add to bookmarks... to add the link to the web browser.

Add to bookmarks option

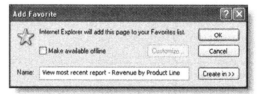 **Add to bookmarks** – adds a link to your browser bookmarks or favorites which allows you to access the report directly without having to navigate through Cognos Connection.

This displays a dialog box from the browser confirming the new link in the bookmarks. Click OK to save the link in your bookmarks or favorites list.

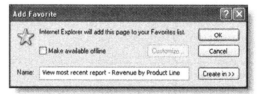

MS Internet Explorer confirmation for new Favorite

More on scheduling

Because scheduling is a very important feature of Cognos Connection, it will be discussed in more detail in the next chapter.

7

Chapter 7: Scheduling BI Objects

Cognos 8 BI provides powerful features for report scheduling and distribution. Reports can be scheduled to automatically execute and distribute to multiple destinations in multiple formats. Advanced options include the capability of creating a single report that will be executed, and its contents automatically divided and distributed to interested parties.

Schedule Reports

One of the most powerful features of Cognos 8 BI is its integrated scheduling and report distribution options.   This chapter focuses on these options.

Saving multiple report output versions

By default, to save storage space on the server, only one report output version is stored in Cognos Connection. This option is very simple to modify by resetting the report properties.

1. Click on the Set Properties icon (circled below) of the report to modify its properties.

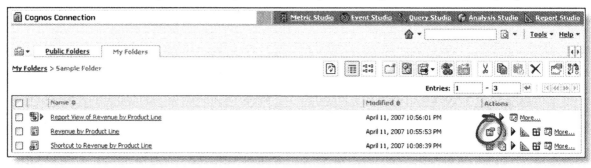

Set Properties option

2. Modify the number of occurrences (1) and press OK (2) to store the new values.

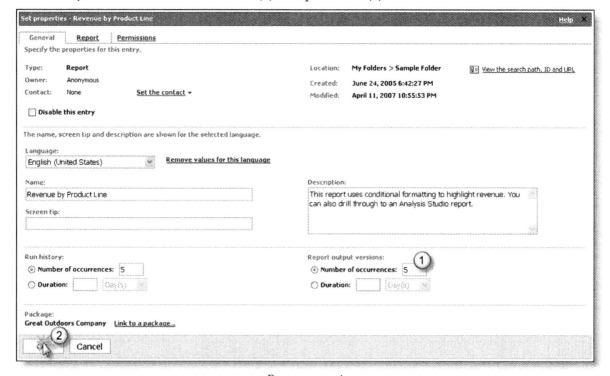

Report properties

Scheduling a report

The scheduling of reports allows for the batch generation of reports, and can be used to make better use of the available infrastructure by generating long-running reports during off-peak or low-load hours. The reports can be scheduled to run and be saved to the portal, sent by email or printed automatically in multiple formats and/or languages.

1. Click on the Schedule option (circled below) to access the scheduling properties.

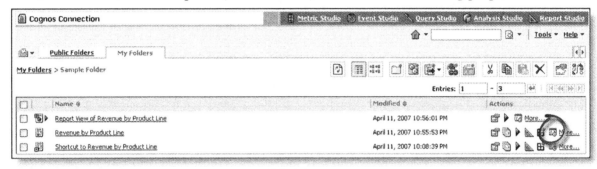

Schedule option

Schedule – allows for batch generation of reports or jobs.

In the schedule page, specify the frequency of execution, the options (format and language of the report and its delivery mechanism) and any prompt values needed.

If a report is missing a required parameter, it will fail with a missing parameter error message. To avoid this, you have to choose values for any required prompt where no default value was previously specified.

Later on, you will see how you can avoid these error messages using Report Views to execute the same report with multiple default values.

---

2. Schedule the report to run every 1 minute for 5 minutes to understand the scheduling process. Just select By Day (1), select Every 1 minute (2), End by (3) and specify the time it should finish scheduling (4). Press OK to create the schedule.

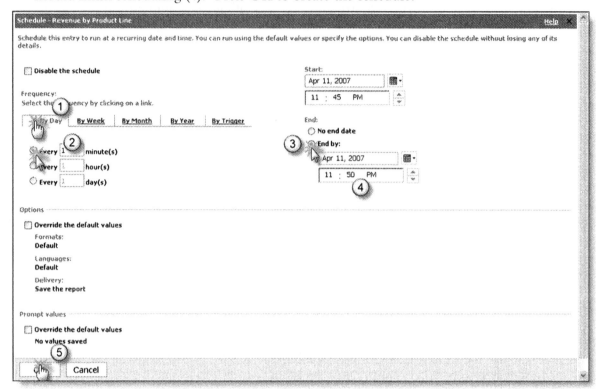

Scheduling a report

This will create the schedule and take you back to Cognos Connection.

You can select the "override the default values" option in the Options section to specify additional actions for the report. There you can specify the formats and delivery methods that you want the report to generate. You are not restricted to one value, but can choose as many formats or methods as you need.

The options that you can specify include:

- Formats: HTML, PDF, several Excel formats and XML.

- Languages: English, German, French and Japanese are the standard languages available. Other can be included with the optional Supplementary Languages installation.

- Delivery mechanism: Save the report to Cognos Connection as output or report view; Print it or send it as an email (additional options for email are to include the report as an attachment or just to include the link to the report in Cognos Connection).

The page to override the default values is:

Overriding the default values

Once the report is scheduled, an advanced tool will let you monitor the status of scheduled objects.

Monitoring a scheduled report

The Schedule Management option is available via Tools menu in Cognos Connection. The tool allows for monitoring and managing of schedules.

Monitoring activities

To monitor activities, you should:

1. Select the Schedule Management option (2) from the Tools menu (1) at Cognos Connection.

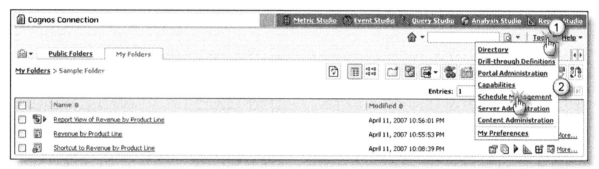

Schedule Management option

This displays the Schedule Management page where jobs can be monitored and a complete status of run activities can be accessed.

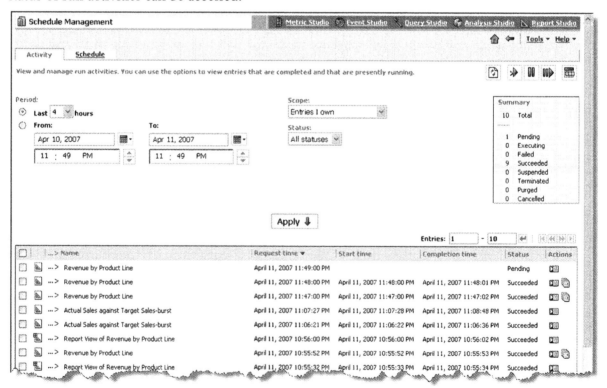

Schedule Management page

You can manage pending activities by using available options such as:

      Cancel – used to cancel pending activities.

      Suspend – used to suspend pending activities.

      Release – used to release (continue) suspended activities.

View future activities

You can access the list of future scheduled activities by accessing the View future activities window.

2. Click on the View future activities icon (circled below) to access the outstanding scheduled activities.

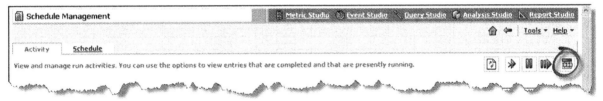

View future activities option

      View future activities – display outstanding scheduled activities.

From this page, you can see scheduled activities, cancel them or even schedule new ones.

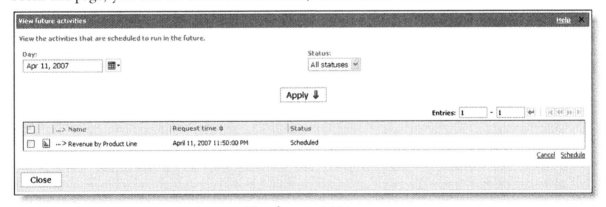

View future activities page

Close this page to go back to Schedule Management.

View execution history

From the list of activities in Schedule Management, we can see the reports that were executed, when they were executed, how long they took to execute as well as their execution status.

Viewing scheduled activities

Notice that there are some actions, at the right, that we can perform for each activity.

View run history

The **View run history details** option in the Schedule Management shows historic information. This option can be selected directly from Cognos Connection, but a link is also provided here.

3. Click on the View run history details icon (circled below) to view the report execution details.

View run history details option

This will display the View run history details page.

4.   Click on Yes (circled below) below Report Outputs to see the generated output versions.

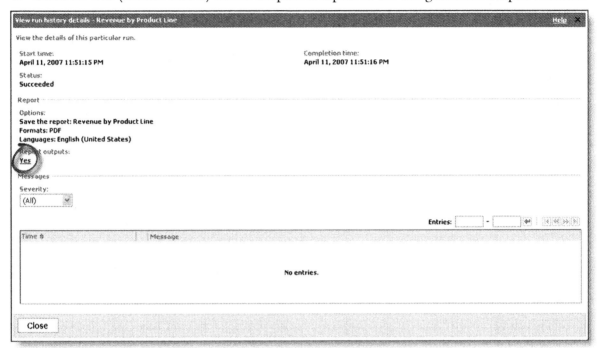

View run history – details

This displays the View report output versions page with the list of generated reports.

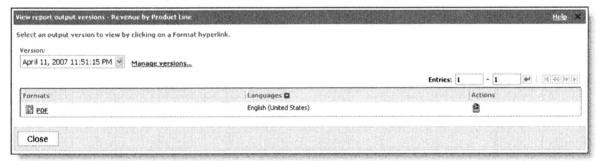

View report output versions

Press Close to return to Schedule Management.

View report outputs

The View report outputs option in Schedule Management shows output versions. It is a shortcut to access the report output without having to go through the history details. This can also be accessed directly from the report actions at Cognos Connection.

5. Click on the View report outputs icon (circled below) to view the list of available report output versions.

View report output option

This displays the View report output versions page. Here you may see a list of available report outputs, which can be accessed by clicking the icons.

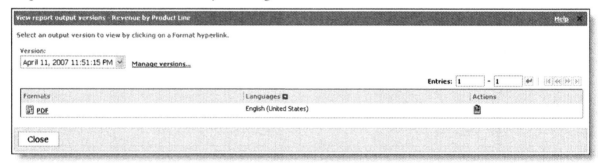

View report output page

Press Close to return to Schedule Management.

View scheduled activities

The second tab in Schedule Management shows the activities scheduled for execution. Here you can see scheduled activities with the most common available actions.

1. After selecting the Schedule tab, click on More... (circled below) to see all the available options for scheduled activities.

Schedule activities page

This displays the Perform an action page for the selected activity.

2. Click on View report output versions (circled below) to see the actual report outputs.

Perform an action page

This should show the View report output versions page that provides the latest output.

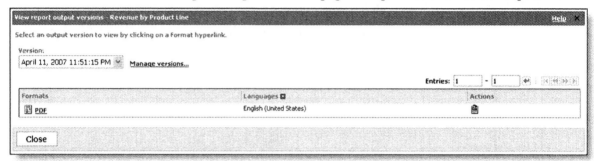

View report output version page

This is the same option seen before, but in this case, we are going to get additional details from the different versions we have stored.

3. Click on the list below Version to see the additional available report output versions.

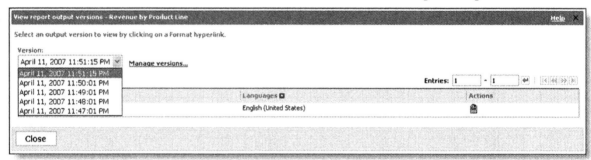

Viewing list of available versions

There are several versions in the drop-down list above because we modified the properties of the report to save five versions instead of only one, which is the standard. You can use the Manage versions… option to modify this option.

4. Press Manage versions… to perform operations on the different versions.

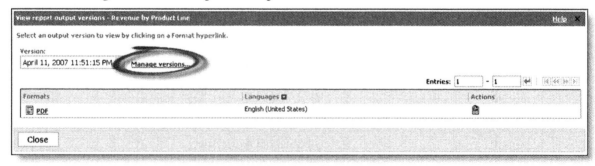

Manage list of available versions

This should provide a list of the available versions with run time information. You can now select versions and delete them. Click Close to go back to the actions menu.

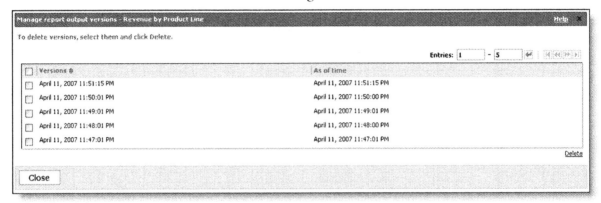

List of report output versions

Scheduling with parameters

Scheduling can be done directly for any report without parameters. If a report with required parameters is scheduled without proper values, it will show in the execution history as "failed to run due to missing parameters". To overcome this issue, you can store parameter values in a report at a scheduled time. If you have multiple reports that you want to schedule and they require parameters, you can create Report Views for each option, store the specific parameter values of each one, and then schedule the Report View. This is what we will demonstrate.

Let us use the report Revenue by Sales Branch. This report asks you to specify the country for which you want to run the report, so we will create a Report View with the value stored for successful execution by the schedule.

1. Look for the report Revenue by Sales Branch in the Report Studio Report Samples folder in the Great Outdoors Company package in the Public Folders tab. Choose the Create a Report View option (circled below).

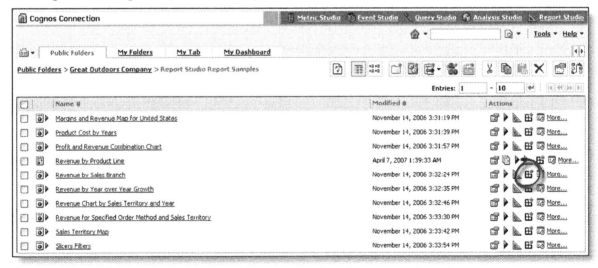

Looking for the report

This launches the New Report View wizard.

2. Save the Report View in the Sample Folder in the My Folders tab.

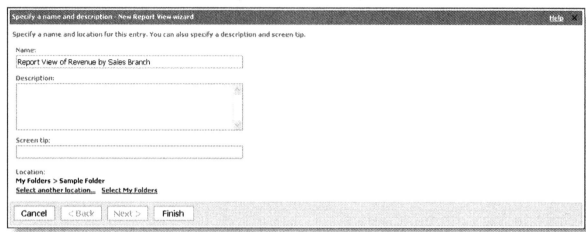

Creating the report view

This should create the report view in the Sample Folder.

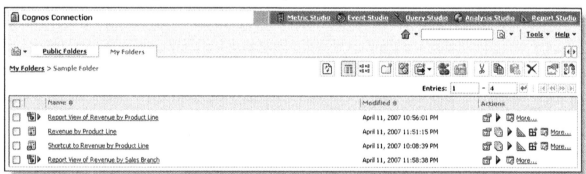

List of entries in the Sample Folder

As you can see, the available actions are restricted to those for a Report View.

3. Click on the report view to execute the report.

Executing the report view

By default, this report will display a prompt requesting a value for Country. The report filters the data by the chosen value.

4.   Choose United States and press OK to execute.   (OK is disabled until you choose a value).

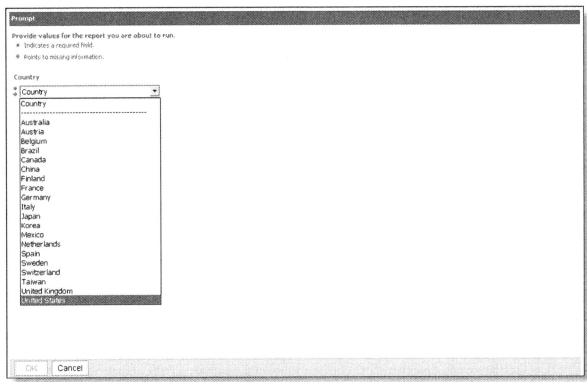

Choosing a value from a prompt

The report is then executed and filtered for the selected value.

Report run with United States as the selected country.

As it is set up right now, every time you click on the report view it will ask you for a value. If you schedule the report to run without choosing a value, it will execute with errors, as shown below.

Expected error message for a scheduled report without required parameters

To correct issues with scheduling, the properties of the report view can be modified to include the value.

5.   Click on Set properties... to include the value.

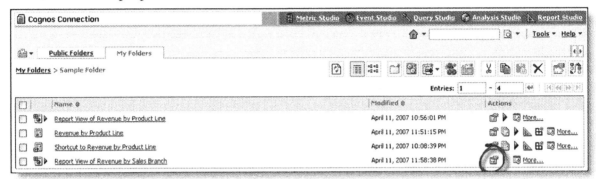

Modify the report view properties

In Set properties, remember that the first page is for General information, and the last one is for Permissions. However, we want to modify the page regarding specific report view properties, which is the middle page.

6.   Click on the Report view tab for the object-specific properties.

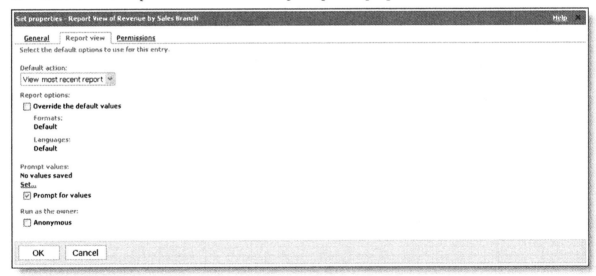

Report view specific properties

We want to modify the Prompt Values so that instead of using the Prompt for values option to request selection from the list of values, we can set a specific value for the report view.

7.   Click on Set... (circled below) to assign the specific value to the properties.

Modify the report view properties

This will immediately look at the report and display prompts so we can specify our desired values.

8.   Open up the list and choose United States. Press OK when ready.

Choosing a value from the list

By choosing the value, we are able to see it under Prompt Values (see next image). We will no longer have to prompt for values, as the value is already selected.

9. Press OK to go back to Cognos Connection. (Remember to clear the Prompt for values option).

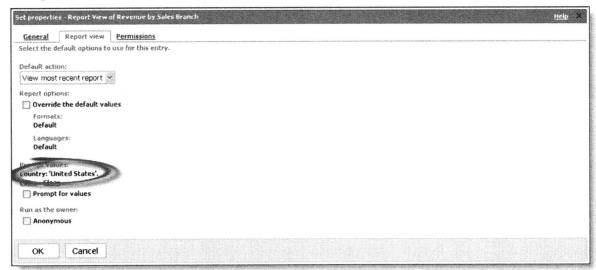

Properties with a selected prompt value

The report view now has a selected value, so it can be executed without prompting for values.

10. Click on the report view.

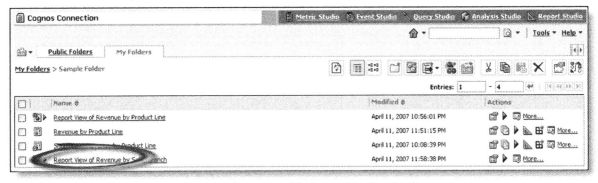

Execute the report with the newly selected value

Notice that the report generated automatically without prompting for any values.

Executed report

This means that the report is ready for scheduling because it does not require any interaction. This demonstration should give you an idea of how you can create several other report views for other countries, so other countries will also receive the report automatically using the Scheduler.

> *Although this may seem like a simple way to schedule parameter-based reports, if you have many options scheduled, it may get quite complicated in terms of maintenance. Cognos 8 BI has a powerful option called Bursting that allows for the generation of a single report where the system will automatically break it in pieces where desired (called "bursting") and distribute it accordingly.*

Press Go back to return to Cognos Connection.

Scheduling multiple reports

In some cases, we may need to schedule a large number of reports at the same time; let us say we need to run reports on Sales for multiple countries. You can do this by scheduling each report view individually, or you can create a job that will group multiple entries, but can be scheduled in just one step.

The **Job** is another type of object that we can store in Cognos Connection.

1. Click on the New job option (circled below) to create a new job specification.

New Job option

New job – used to create new job specifications

This should bring up the New Job Wizard page.

2. Enter the name, description, screen tip and location for the new job specification. Be sure to save it in the Sample Folder in My Folders. Press Next to continue with the wizard.

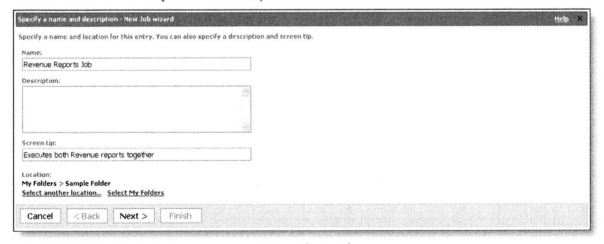

New Job wizard

This displays the Select the steps page on which you specify the steps that the job will execute. This may be reports and/or other jobs that you want to execute at the same time, concurrently or in sequence (one after the other).

3. Click Add... (circled below) to select the report that you want to include in the job.

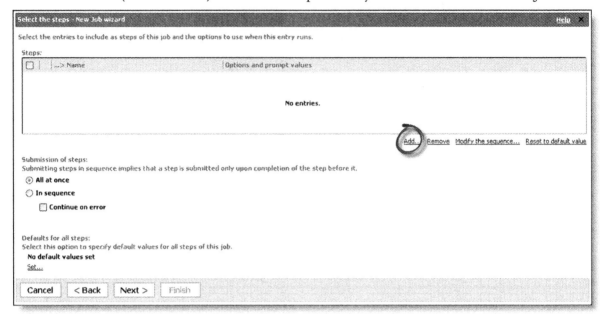

Adding steps to the job

The Add option should present you with a navigator that allows you to select the entries that you want to add to the job.

4. Let's say that we want to select all entries in the Sample Folder. Click on the Select All option (1), press the Add button (2) to include them in the Selected entries list, and then press OK (3) to go back to the job specification.

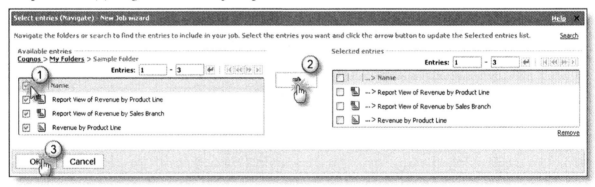

Selecting entries as job steps

This should add multiple steps to the new job specification. Steps can be executed All at once or In sequence. If you run In sequence, you have to specify what to do if one of the steps fails. If there are no dependencies upon steps, you can choose to Continue on error.

"All at once" may slow down a system if executing multiple, large steps concurrently.

You can also specify defaults for all steps; for example, a specific format or language, as when you schedule a report.

5.   Click on In sequence (1) and press Next (2) to continue.

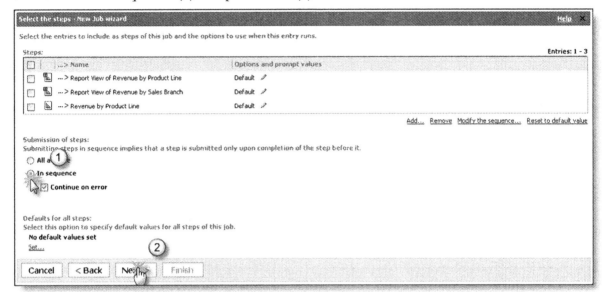

Executing steps in sequence

After choosing the steps and how are they going to be executed, we have to choose what to do with the job. You can Save it and run it once when you press Finish. Alternatively, it can be saved and scheduled for execution later, or you can save it without executing it.

6.   Press Finish to use the default Save and run once.

Choosing the job execution

Because we selected our report to run once, it displays the Run with options page. This is the same as choosing the Run with options page from Cognos Connection. Notice that it lists the steps to be executed.

7. Press Run to execute.

Execute the job

This will show a confirmation page if it was not previously disabled in the preferences.

8. Press OK to execute.

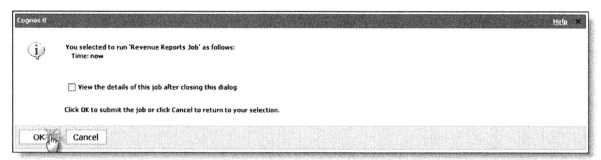

Confirming the Execution

Pressing OK should bring us back to Cognos Connection. Notice that we have a new entry in the Sample Folder with the specific job icon and that the Run with options icon (circled below) is available.

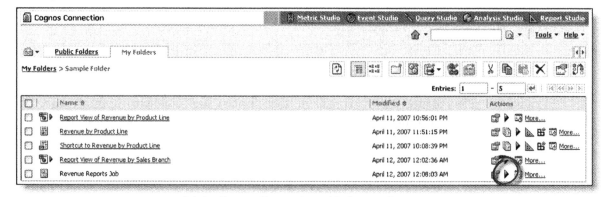

Job in Cognos Connection with Run with options

Monitoring the job

Since we know that we requested to execute the job once, we can monitor the job by using the Schedule Manager.

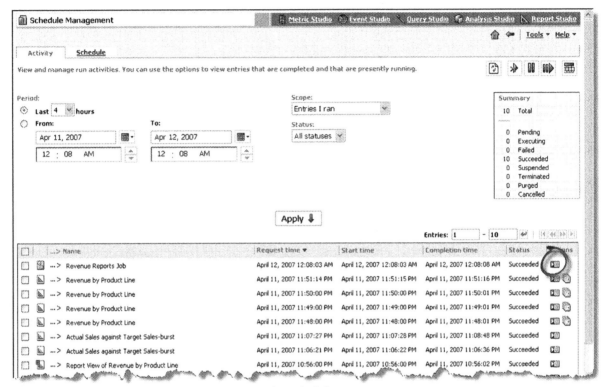

Job in the Schedule Manager

Here, we can see the status of the job. Notice that the View run history details option is available to view the details of the execution.

9.   Press the View run history details to view the execution status.

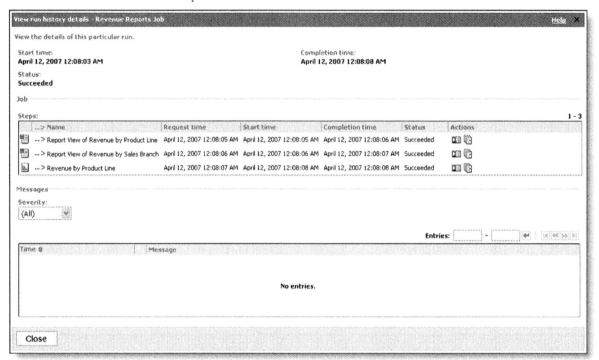

View run history details for a job

As you can see, the history shows all the steps of the job with the usual execution information, including links to more details and to the report outputs.

Advanced report distribution using bursting

As previously mentioned, Cognos 8 BI allows for the configuration of reports in such a way that a report can be broken down in parts, and these parts can be distributed to specific recipients by any delivery method we choose. This is called Report Bursting, and it is a very powerful feature of Cognos 8 BI.

For bursting to work, some setup has to be done in the report when the Report Author creates it. The Consumer is then able to execute the report by activating a bursting property, and the report will then get generated, bursted and delivered accordingly.

To show this functionality, we will use a report that has been pre-configured to be available for bursting. If we run the report without activating the bursting option, it will execute like any other report.

1. Click on the report called Actual Sales against Target Sales-burst in the folder Report Studio Report Samples, at the GO Sales and Retailers package in Public Folders.

Sample bursting report

As the report is run with the default options, it is supposed to generate as any other report. The report starts with a cover page, and in the following page you get the actual data.

2. Page down to see the actual data in the report.

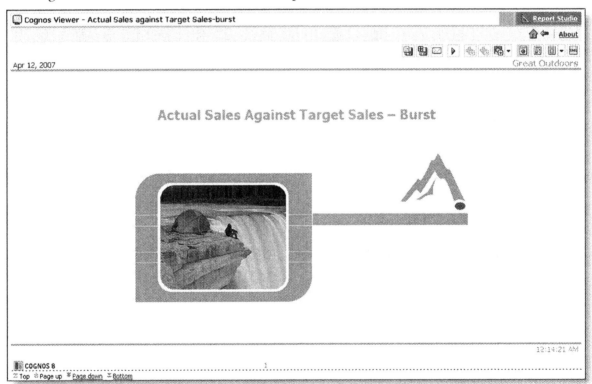

Sample bursting report cover page

Here you can see the actual data, which is a comparison by Staff Name for several years of the Sales Target vs. the Actual Revenue, and shows the differences.

3.   Press the Return icon to go back to Cognos Connection.

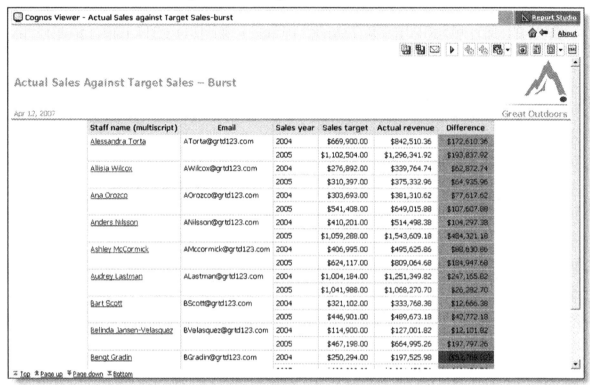

Sample bursting report data

Back in Cognos Connection, we will now execute the same report again, but this time with the bursting option activated.

4.   Click on Run with options (circled below) to activate the bursting option.

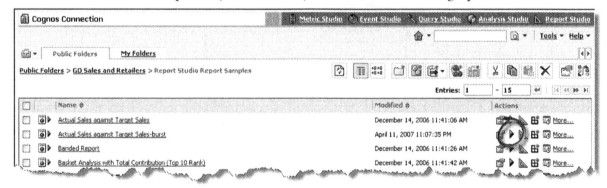

Run with options to activate bursting

Initially, you will get the basic Run with options page. As bursting is an advanced option, we need the advanced options link.

5.   Click on advanced options (shown below) to activate bursting.

Run with options basic options

The last option at the bottom right corner of the next page is Bursting. We have seen this page before, but that option was not displayed because the previous report we used was not configured for bursting.

6. Click on Burst the report (1) to activate the bursting option. By default, the system is supposed to select Save the report (2), so just press Run (3).

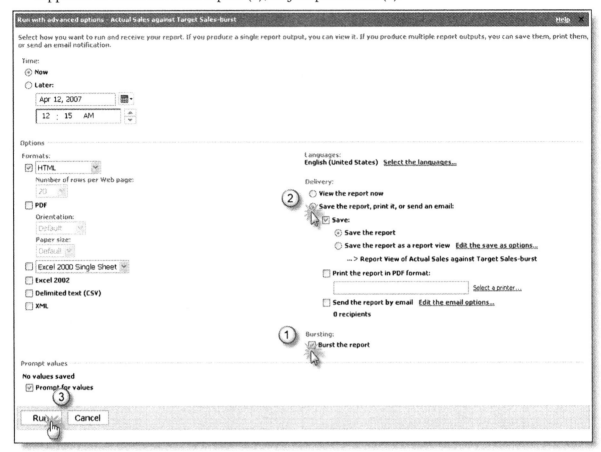

Running a bursted report

Once you press Run, you will get a confirmation page.

7. Click OK to continue.

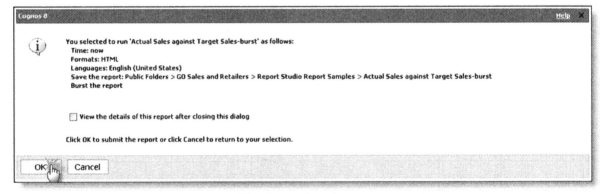

Bursting confirmation page

The report will execute, and depending on the available system hardware, you may have to press Refresh several times until the report is available at Cognos Connection. Once it is ready, you will see the View report output icon available among the report actions.

8.   Click on View report output (circled below) to see the bursted output.

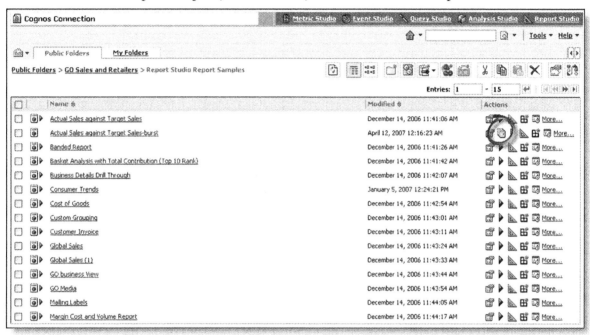

Asking for the bursting output

You should be able to see that the report was generated multiple times, once per each staff member. This means that the report was bursted by the criterion of "staff member" and stored in Cognos Connection as specified in the Run options. Let us see the output for some of the staff members.

9.   Click on the HTML link for Alessandra Torta.

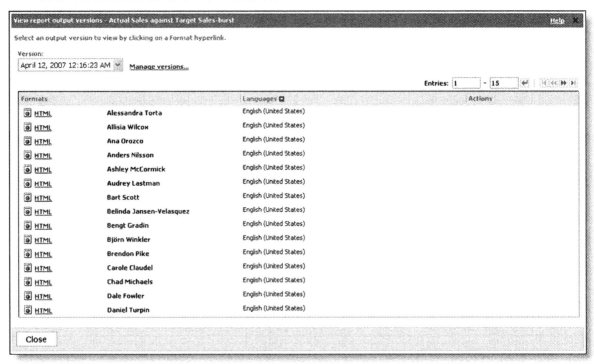

List of report outputs

This should show the stored report output for Alessandra Torta. As with the unbursted version of the report we saw originally, the initial page is just a cover page.

10. Move the scrollbar down to see additional data.

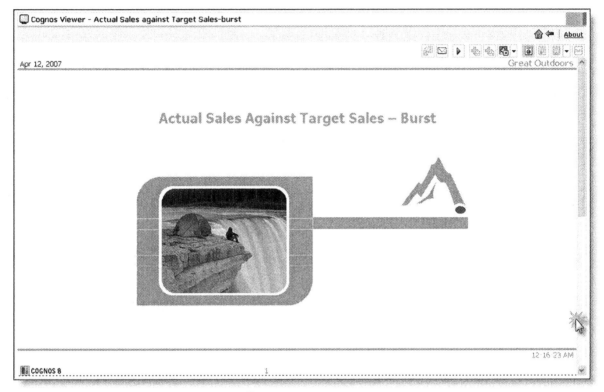

Report output cover page

When we scroll down the report, we see that some data is available. Notice that in this case the only available data is for Alessandra Torta. The report output was stored in Cognos Connection, but the same output could have been delivered by email or to a printer.

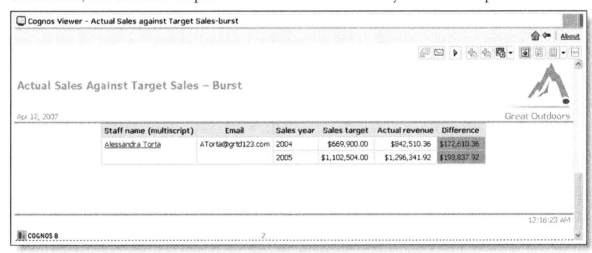

Bursted report showing data for Alessandra Torta

If you go back to the list and choose another person, let's say Allisia Wilcox, you will get the initial cover page followed by the data for Allisia Wilcox only.

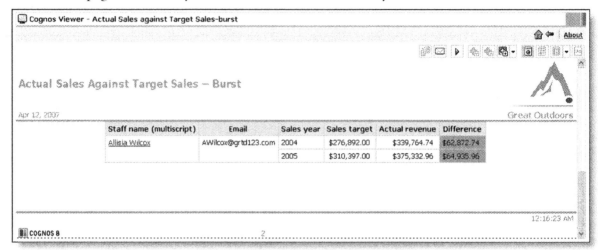

Bursted report showing data for Allisia Wilcox

By generating only one report with the bursting option activated, we are able to see how Cognos breaks the report into multiple sections, thus providing a powerful distribution capability.

Customizing your environment

Now that we have seen the available capabilities for Cognos 8 BI Objects, we can also modify our working environment to make it more productive by creating pages with exactly the functionality that we want to be more accessible to us. In the next chapter, we will discuss the multiple available options to modify the Cognos Connection portal.

8

Chapter 8: Customizing the Portal

Cognos Connection provides multiple preferences to enhance the user experience. These preferences range from standard options for languages, currencies and regionalization to the user-defined creation of pages and tabs to enhance the default Cognos Connection navigation.

Preferences

Users, based on their individual preferences, can personalize the Cognos Connection interface. By changing your preferences, you can modify the standard look and feel of the portal, change how you want Cognos Connection to display available entries, and alter other personal preferences to suit your needs.

Accessing Preferences

The Preferences are easily accessible through the Tools menu at the main Cognos Connection page.

1. Click on Tools (circled below), then on My Preferences.

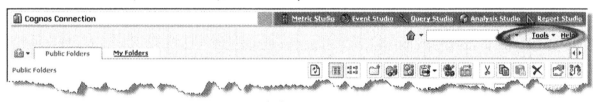

Accessing Tools from Cognos Connection

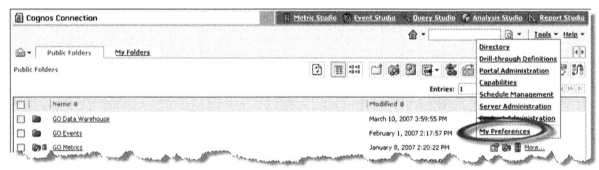

Selecting My Preferences

This will display the Set Preferences page.

Within the Set Preferences function, there are three tabs or pages from which to choose:

*   General preferences

*   Personal preferences

*   Portal Tabs preferences

Let us look at each one.

The **General** tab is used to customize general preferences that will modify the standard look and feel of the portal. There are preferences to change the layout of Cognos Connection, the language used in the page displays, the style (look and feel) that Cognos Connection will adopt, and the number of entries to display. There are also preferences for the format of the default report output and the automatic refresh rate, and options that let you avoid additional informational pages such as the Welcome Page and the Summary when you select Run with options.

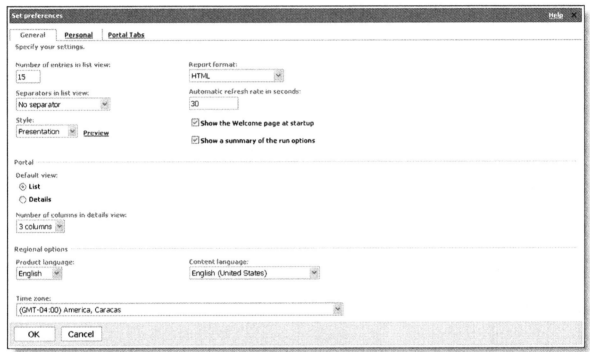

My Preferences – General tab

The second tab is for **Personal** information. This contains user-specific information for the user who is connected to Cognos Connection. In our case, because we are not using security and are connecting as an Anonymous user, the Personal page has several empty fields. When Cognos 8 BI is configured to access an authentication source, the information from the user authentication (i.e., user sign-on) is displayed.

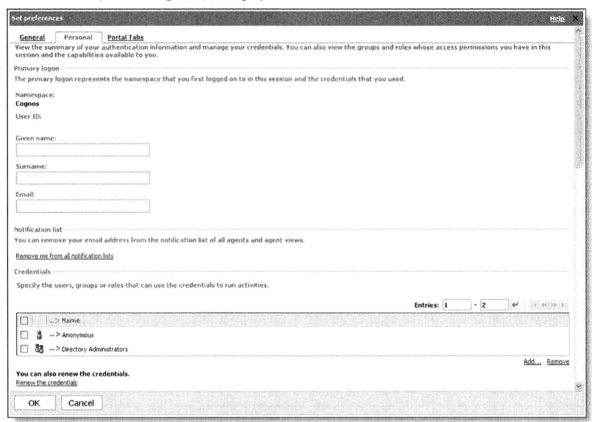

My Preferences – Personal tab – I

Additionally, we see information on this tab that refers to "credentials". We can assign or "lend" our credentials to other users, permitting them to execute reports; this is where we can specify which users, groups or roles will be able to use our credentials.

Here is an example of how this might work. Let us say that you have a report that accesses a database that only *you* have access to; with the credentials preference in Cognos Connection, you can create a report with some dynamic filters that will only provide the "need-to-know" information to users who need to run the report by using your credentials to connect to the database.

Scrolling down in this same page, you can see some additional security information. You can see which groups/roles you belong to and which capabilities (such as Bursting) you have access to.

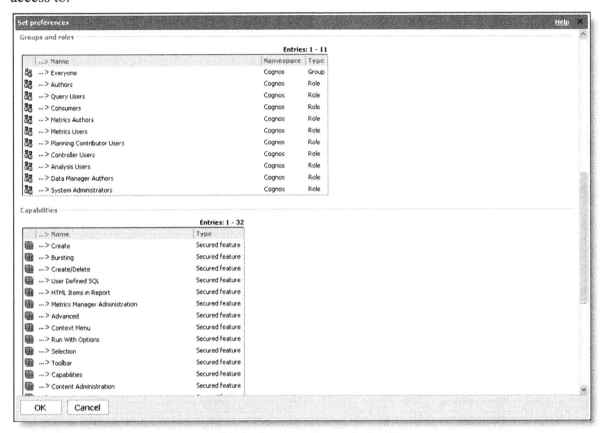

My Preferences – Personal tab – II

The final preferences tab, **Portal Tabs,** controls which navigation tabs you want to see in the Cognos Connection portal. By default, you can see there are two options, Public Folders and My Folders. Later in the book, we will show you how to add more tabs to your environment.

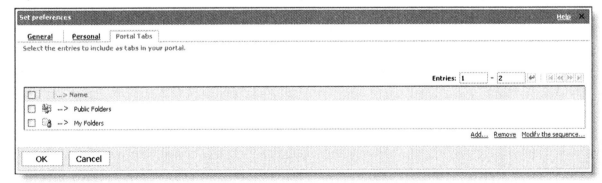

My Preferences – Portal Tabs

By modifying the sequence of the tabs, you can select which tab you want to show by default when connecting to Cognos Connection. Let us see how changing the preferences can affect the system's look and feel.

Modifying Preferences

To demonstrate how the preferences impact the portal, let us make some modifications and then access the portal again to see the effect of our changes.

1. In the General tab, modify the preferences by changing the portal's Default view and select French as the new default language.

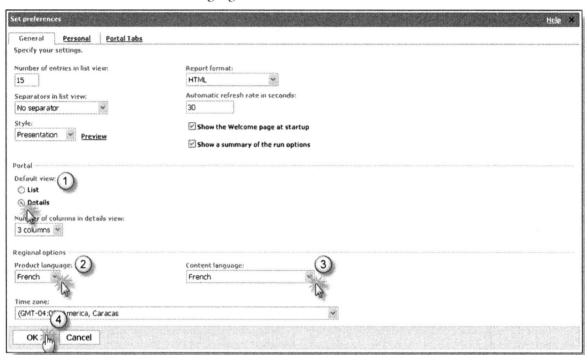

Modifying the preferences

Voila! The portal now shows the entries in three columns with details (see example below). In addition, we observe that not only have the interface options changed to French, but also the content itself.

For the content to change, the information has to be manually entered for each object in its properties. Cognos 8 BI will not translate content; it will display what has been defined for each language on each object.

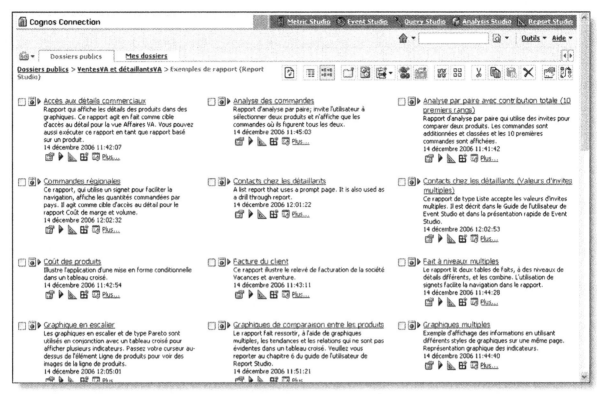

Cognos Connection in French

2.   Change it back to English by going to the Tools ("Outils") menu and choosing the last option My Preferences ("Mes préférences").

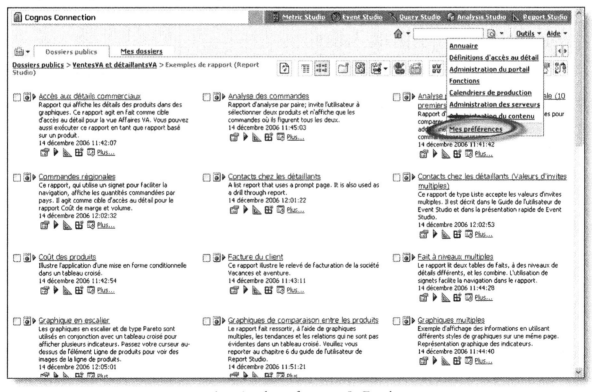

Accessing the preferences – In French

3. On the "Général" tab, change the language to English ("Anglais") and press OK.

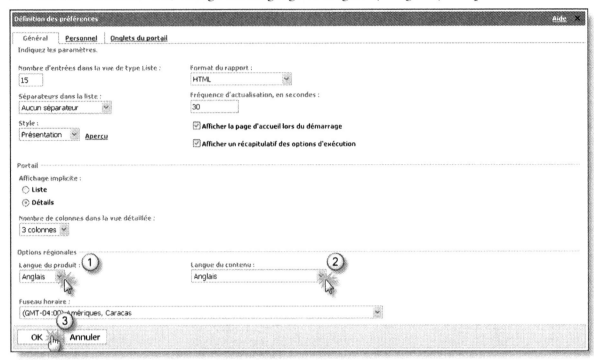

Set Preferences – In French

Cognos Connection now returns to an English-language display.

Managing Navigation Tabs

By default, Cognos Connection has only two Navigation tabs in the portal: one to access the Public Folders and another for My Folders. Cognos Connection is flexible enough to let us add additional tabs and customize them as we wish. We can even choose which tab we want to see as our default when connecting to Cognos Connection. This allows for the creation of a dashboard page with our desired objects to be displayed immediately upon connecting to Cognos Connection. This can save time when you have reports or objects you need to access regularly.

To set up your own personal "dashboard" in Cognos Connection, you first need to create something called **Pages**, which you can then add to the Tab Navigator.

Creating Pages

Pages can be easily created and customized.

1. Click on the New Page icon (circled below) to access the page-building utility, called the New Page wizard.

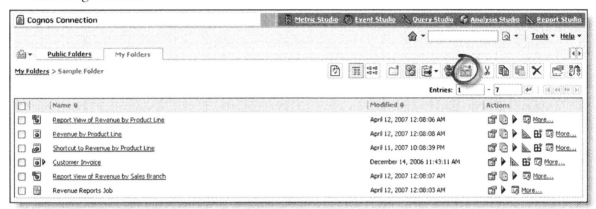

New Page option

New Page – used to create new pages to be used as tabs.

2. Enter the name, description, screen tip and location for the new page. Be sure you save it in the Sample Folder in My Folders. Press Next to continue with the wizard.

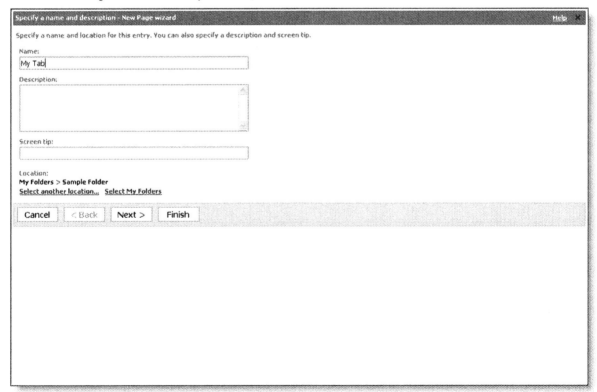

New Page wizard – Name and description

The next page asks you to choose the number of columns that you want the page to have. By default, it will show just one, which is perfect if you are creating the page to be used as a dashboard showing a report.

New Page wizard - Set columns and layout

In our case, we are going to build a more complex page taking advantage of available Cognos utilities.

3. Choose a layout with two columns (1). The first one should take 30% of the page real estate (2) and the other one the other available 70% (3). Press next to continue.

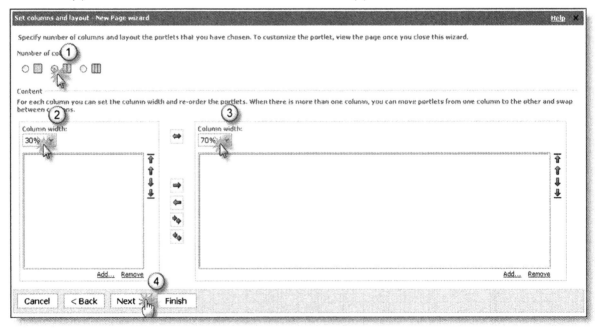

New Page wizard – Configuring our page

The next page specifies some Page Style information, such as titles, borders, bars and others. For now, use the defaults. We will make other modifications to styles later on.

4. Click next to continue.

New Page wizard – Page style

The last page in the wizard lets you Select actions for your page by asking if you want to add the page to the portal tabs automatically, and if you want to see the page. We will not check these options at the moment because we are doing this the manual way to learn the process; later on, we will use the automatic process.

5. Click Finish to end the wizard.

New Page wizard – Final actions

The wizard should have created a new Page entry in your Cognos Connection portal. If you look at the entries, you will see that you now have a new "My Tab" entry in the Sample Folder (see next image).

Customizing Pages

Now that we have created the new page, we have to modify it to add content.

1. Click on My Tab to view the page.

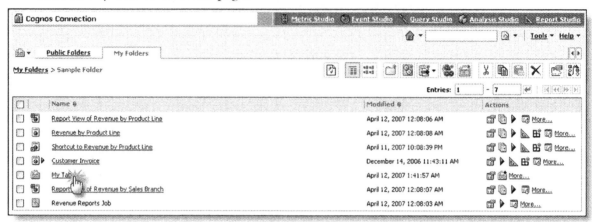

View My Tab from Cognos Connection

This brings up the page in Cognos Viewer. As the page does not have any content (yet), you should see an empty page. We will now customize it to include content.

2. Click on the Edit icon (circled below) in the Cognos Viewer toolbar.

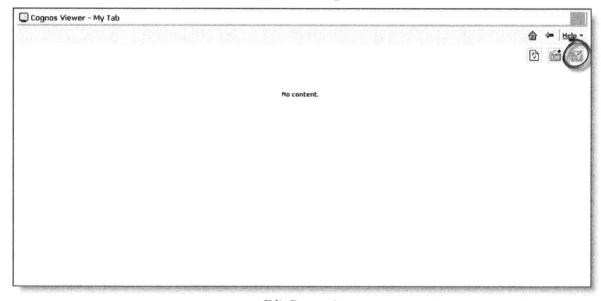

Edit Page option

  Edit Page – used to customize pages.

This brings up a Set Properties page for My Tab. By default, it will show the Layout and Content tab we created earlier, where we can now add content to the page columns.

3. Press the Add... option (circled below) under the left-hand column to add content to this area.

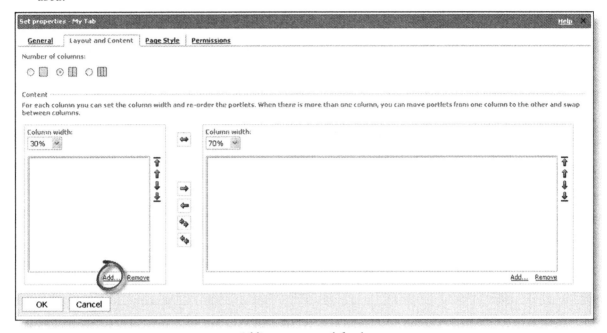

Adding content to left column

This displays the Portlet navigator. A **portlet** is a small application that can be added as content to pages. Portlets can present both Cognos internal data as well as external content by using URLs to access outside sources. They can also be customized to integrate with other customer applications.

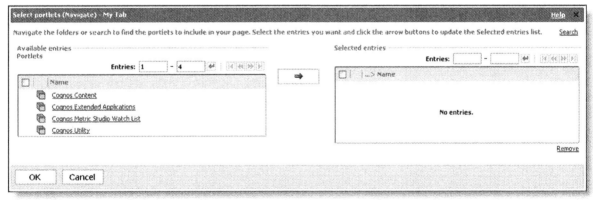

Portlet Navigator

4. Click on Cognos Content. From there, choose Cognos Navigator and Cognos Search (1) as two portlets you want to add to the page column. Click the right arrow (2) to include your choices in the Selected Entries list. Press OK to continue (3).

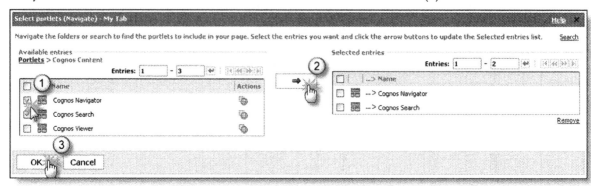

Choosing desired content

By pressing OK, we return to page properties where the two portlets should now be added to the left column, as shown below. The Cognos Navigator portlet allows us to navigate through the entire Cognos Connection folder structure, starting from either Public Folders or My Folders and navigating to any available report. (Of course, if security is enabled, the system will only show those entries you are authorized to see.) Cognos Search is the Search option that will be available from the new Page as well.

Now we need to configure the right side column.

5. Click on the Add... option below the right column (circled below).

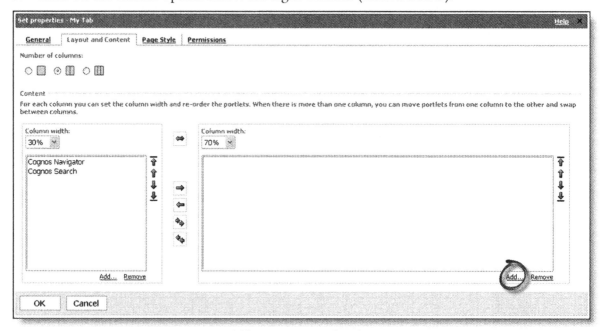

Adding content to right column

Back in the portlet navigator, choose the Cognos Viewer portlet. A Cognos Viewer portlet allows all the functionality of the full Cognos Viewer inside the right column. What we are setting up is the ability to navigate using the Cognos Navigator that we added in the left column of our new page; select a report from that column, and see the report being executed and displayed in the right column.

6.   Navigate to Cognos Content and select Cognos Viewer. Add it to the "Selected entries" by clicking the right arrow, and press OK to go back to the page's properties page.

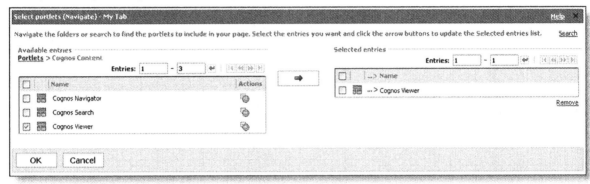

Adding a Cognos Viewer portlet

This completes the configuration of the new page by providing content to both the left and right sides of the page.

7.   Press OK to exit the properties.

This should bring us back to the page itself. The page now displays content in both the left and right sides of the page (see next image). On the left, we see the Cognos Navigator and Cognos Search portlets. On the right, we see an empty (for the moment) Cognos Viewer portlet.

Our main objective is to use our new page to navigate using Cognos Navigator. By clicking on a report, we can have that report display in the Cognos Viewer portlet. There is one additional step that we have to complete to achieve our objective: establishing a connection between Cognos Navigator and Cognos Viewer, so they are aware of each other and can exchange content.

8. Click the Edit option (circled below) in the Cognos Viewer configuration toolbar.

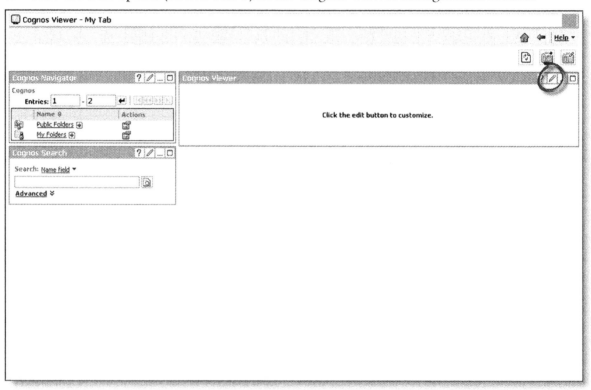

Configuring Cognos Viewer

Now we have access to the properties of the Cognos Viewer within this new page. There are several options to specify the Title of the entry, an option to choose a report to display by default (we will do that soon), the default action to perform, the size of Cognos Viewer in the page and others. Of those, we will focus on one called Channel name that will create a communication channel to this Cognos Viewer to be used by other portlets to send messages and/or content.

9. Name the Channel MyCognosViewer (1). Specify a size of 480 pixels (2) so more of the Cognos Viewer can be seen on the page. Press OK to go back to the page (3).

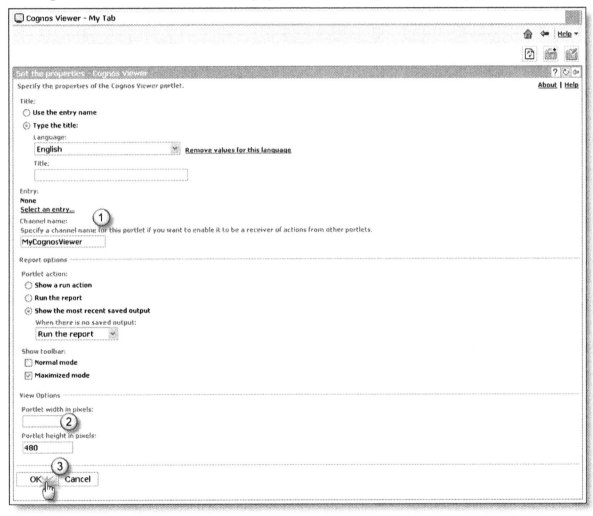

Setting up a Channel

Now that we have named the channel in Cognos Viewer, we have to configure Cognos Navigator to use that channel.

10. Click on the Edit option for Cognos Navigator (circled below).

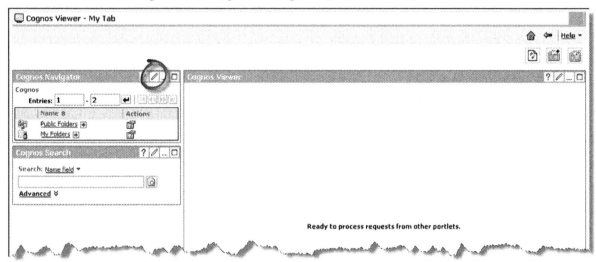

Edit Cognos Navigator properties

The properties for Cognos Navigator should be displayed. Some properties are standard for all portlets, but there are others that depend on a portlet for specific use. In this case, we can configure the folder that should be displayed, how the Cognos Navigator will show the entries, where the navigator is going to display them, and so on. We are focusing on the property for where to Open links, and in our case we want to specify the Cognos Viewer channel that we named MyCognosViewer.

11. Click on "In a destination portlet" (1) and enter the channel name MyCognosViewer (2). Press OK to go back to the page (3).

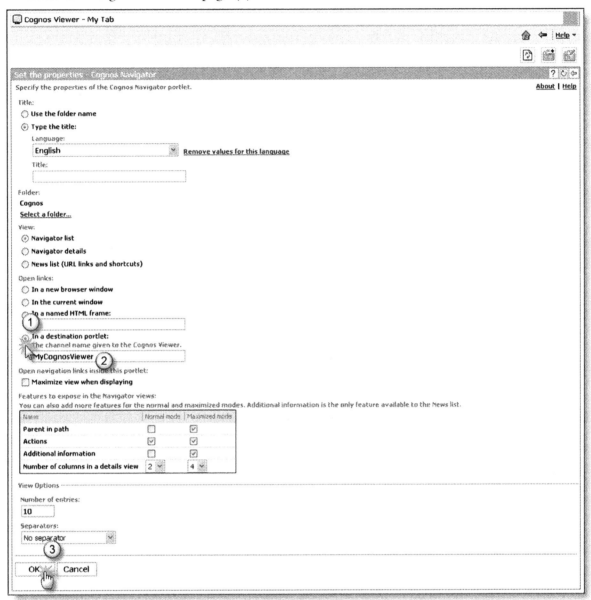

Configuring the Channel

This should complete the configuration. We named a channel in the right-hand column Cognos Viewer and set the properties of the left-hand column Cognos Navigator to point to that channel.

Let us see how it works.

12. Click on Public Folders to navigate through the demo data.

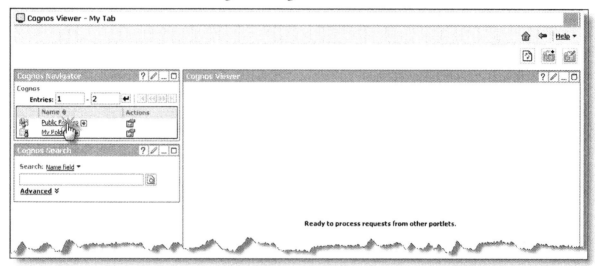

Edit Cognos Navigator properties

This will display the content of the Public Folders the same way as if we were navigating through Cognos Connection (see image below).

13. Click on Great Outdoors Company to list the content of that folder. Subsequently, click on Report Studio Report Samples to list the reports.

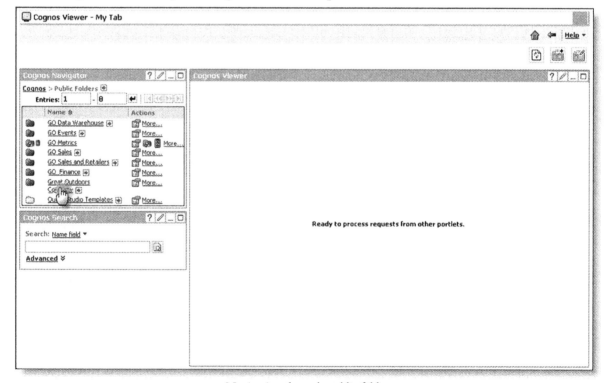

Navigating through public folders

You should see the same list of sample reports we have used throughout the book.

14. Click on the report entitled "Margins and Revenue Map for United States".

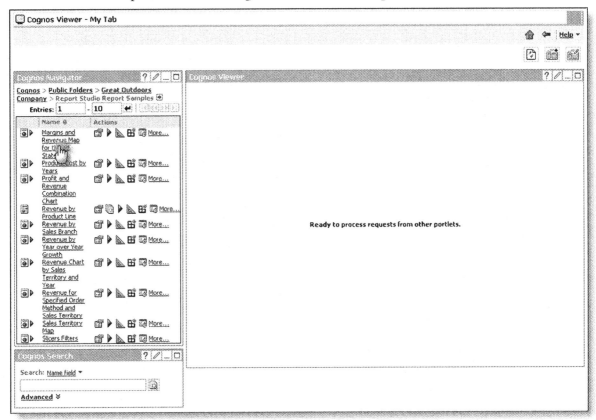

Executing a report from the Cognos Navigator portlet

This should display the available report in the Cognos Viewer portlet on the right side of the page.

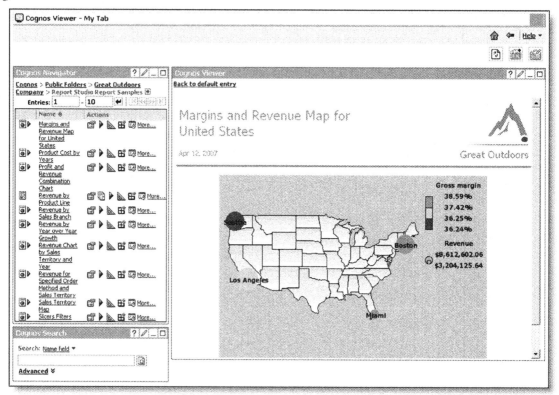

The report running in the Cognos Viewer portlet

Any report that you select from the Cognos Navigator will automatically show in the Cognos Viewer. In the top left corner inside Cognos Viewer you can see a "Back to default entry" link. This should take you back to the initial Cognos Viewer page, which in our case is now empty. We can configure Cognos Viewer to show some content by default, so we do not have the large page left unused.

To this end, we have to get into the Cognos Viewer properties again, but this time we are going to modify the "Entry" property to show a report by default.

15. Click on "Select an entry" (1) and navigate to Public Folders, Great Outdoors Company, Report Studio Report Samples; then select the Sales Territory Map report to show as the default. Press OK (2) to go back to the page.

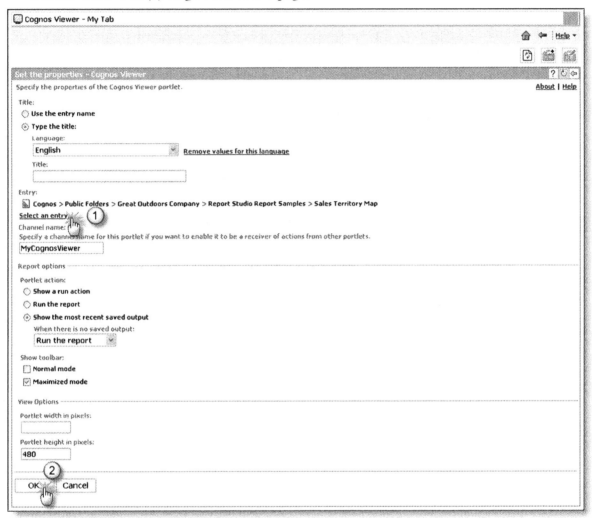

Assigning a default entry for Cognos Viewer

Thus, instead of seeing an empty Cognos Viewer portlet by default, we can immediately see some content making the new page much more attractive and useful.

16. Press the Return option to go back to Cognos Connection.

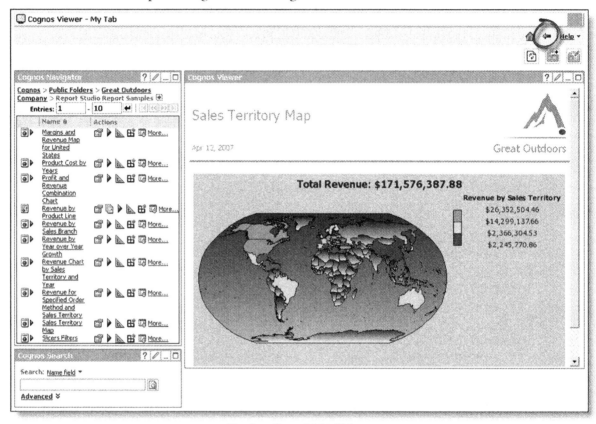

Final configured My Tab page

Adding Pages as Tabs

Now that the page is fully configured, it is time to add it to the Cognos Connection portal. For this, we will use the available Tab Navigator options.

1. Select the Tab Menu (circled below) to modify the portal tabs. Choose the "Add portal tabs…" option to add our page to the tabs.

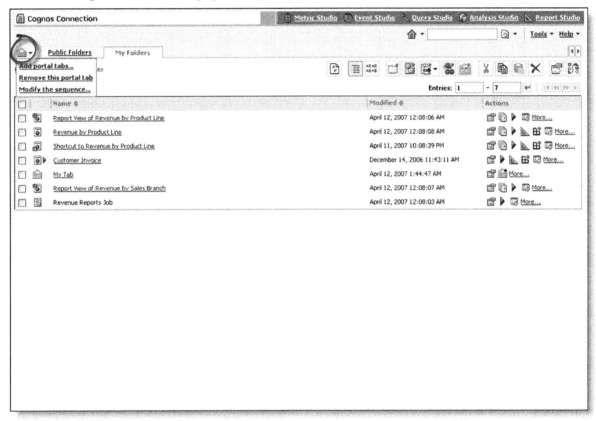

Tab Menu option

 Tab Menu – used to modify the tab structure in Cognos Connection.

A navigator appears, enabling us to choose the page that we want to add.

2. From the Sample Folder in My Folders, choose our newly created page My Tab (1). Click the right arrow to copy our choice to the Selected Entries list (2). Press OK to go back to Cognos Connection (3).

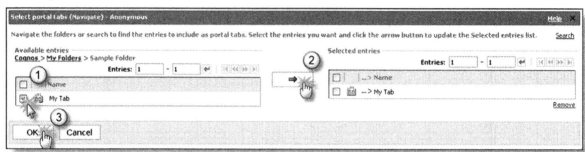

Add My Tab to Cognos Connection tabs

This should add a new tab to Cognos Connection.

3. Click on the tab "My Tab" to access our page from the Tab Navigator.

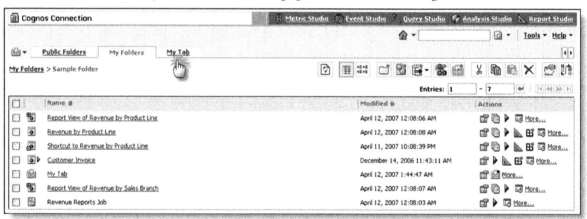

Accessing My Tab from the Tab Navigator

This shows our new page nicely integrated in Cognos Connection. As we have completed our editing, we can now eliminate the edit options from the page so we have a clean interface.

4. Click on the Edit page icon (circled below).

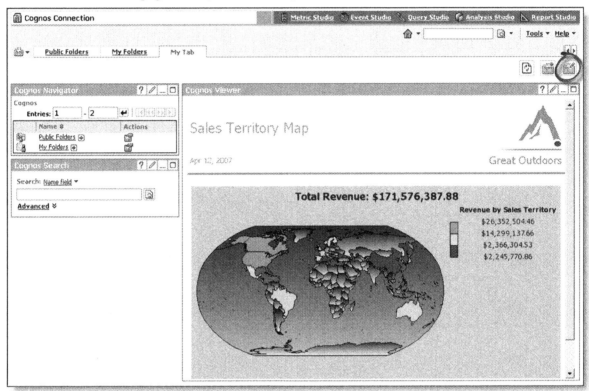

Edit the page properties

Next, from the page properties in the **Page Style** tab, modify the properties to hide any page features that will interfere with a clean look and feel.

5. Select all the Hide options (1, 2, 3) and press OK (4).

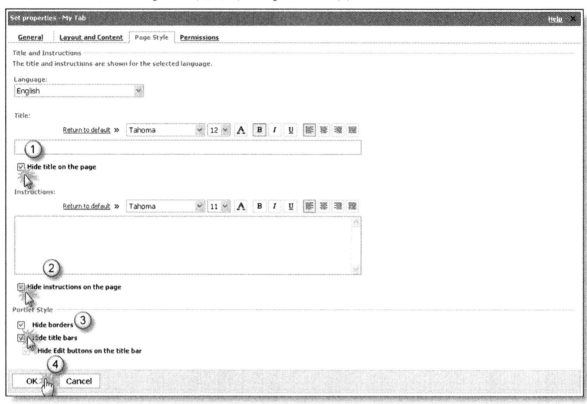

Hide all the page options

The page now displays a clean interface without editing options—a much nicer look and feel.

My Tab without editing options

Creating a Dashboard Page as Tab

We can also add a report as a dashboard to our Cognos Connection interface. This way, the user can set up his or her own page, add it to the tabs and configure it as the default to have quick access to important information.

1. Click on the New Page icon (circled below) to access the page-building utility.

New Page option

This should display the New Page wizard page.

2. Enter the name, description, screen tip and location for the new page specification. Be sure to save it in the Sample Folder in My Folders. Press Next to continue with the wizard.

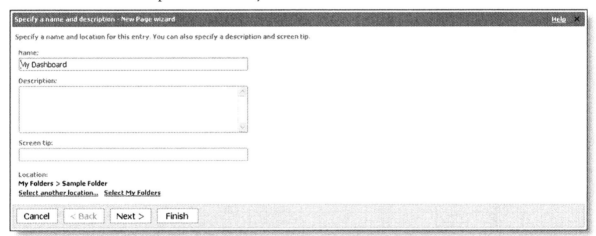

New Page wizard – Name and description

The next page asks you to choose the number of columns that you want the page to display. By default, it will show just one, which is perfect if you are creating the page to be used as a dashboard showing a report.

3. Keep the default option of one column, and choose a Cognos Viewer as Content. (Remember: you have to click on Add… (bottom right corner), navigate to the Cognos Viewer in the available portlets and add it as content as shown in our illustration below). Click Next until you get to the "Select an action" page.

New Page wizard − Configuring our page

The "Select an action" is the last page in the wizard; it asks if you want to add the page to the portal tabs automatically and if you want to see the page.

4. This time, we will select both options, as shown below, and click Finish.

New Page wizard − Final actions

The wizard should have created a new tab in Cognos Connection called "My Dashboard" and automatically added it to the Cognos Connection tabs. Because we have not yet assigned any content to Cognos Viewer, this new page will be empty, but we will provide it with a default report next.

5. Click on Edit option (circled below) in the Cognos Viewer portlet to access the properties.

Access the Cognos Viewer portlet properties

You should see the "Set the properties" page where you can configure all the Cognos Viewer properties. We want to configure the Entry option to display a report in the dashboard page.

6. Press the "Select an entry…" link and navigate until you get the GO Business View report that is available in the Report Studio Report Samples folder in the GO Sales and Retailers package in Public Folders. Press OK to go back to Cognos Connection.

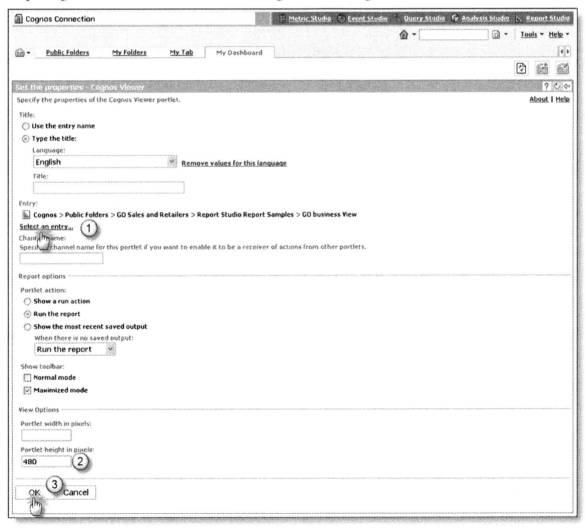

Selecting a report for the Cognos Viewer portlet

Cognos Viewer should now execute and display the specified report. The report that we selected has a cover page and this is something that you may not want to see in a dashboard. When you create your own dashboard in your own Cognos Connection installation, you can modify the report to exclude the initial page in your dashboard.

7. Press the "Page down" link at the bottom left of the page.

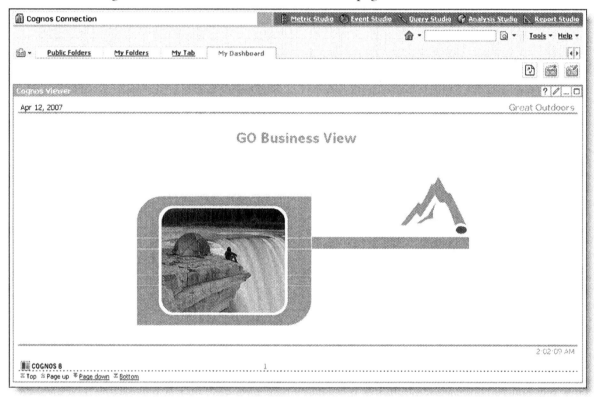

Dashboard cover page

It should now show the dashboard report, which provides important business data on one easily accessible page to which the executive can have easy access from Cognos Connection. Dashboard reports are ideal to show busy executives daily "big picture" information on the state of the business because they can be pre-configured as a default and the executive doesn't have to search through a list of reports to get the information he or she want to see.

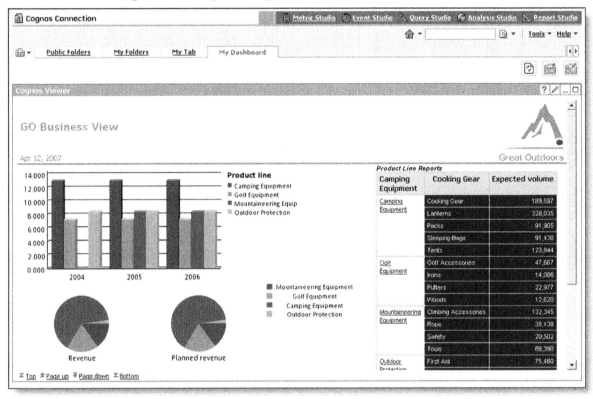

Dashboard – Business View

Setting the default initial tab

You can set a default initial page in your portal by using the Tab Menu's "Modify the Sequence…" option. Just select the tab you want as the initial page, and press "To top" to make it the starting tab. You can also reorder the tabs by using the Up and Down options.

Setting the initial page by default

The order can also be modified in My Preferences by accessing the last tab, Portal Tabs, and choosing the option to "Modify the sequence" at the bottom right corner.

Applying Security to Cognos Connection

Throughout this book, we have followed the examples without security implemented, but in the next chapter, you will be able to see how a secured installation looks.

9

Chapter 9: Security in Cognos Connection

Cognos 8 BI uses security authenticators available within your organization to integrate with your infrastructure. Security authentication supports advanced features, such as Single Sign-on and centralized user management. In this chapter, we will activate security and go through Cognos Connection again to understand how this change will affect the available functionality.

Working with security enabled

Until now, we have worked through our tutorial without using security. In Cognos Connection, security has to be activated by a Cognos Administrator and tied to an authentication source. The authentication source provides Cognos Connection with the user IDs and passwords that Cognos will use to validate users who are attempting to enter the system. In this example, we will configure Cognos 8 BI to access our existing MS Windows XP machine user information. (Your organization may use a different authentication source, and if it is supported by Cognos, Cognos Connection can be configured to work with that as well).

Cognos 8 BI can be configured to have Anonymous and Authenticated access at the same time. Of course, if this is the case, the access available to Anonymous users has to be restricted to the essentials. In the next screenshot, you will see how an Anonymous user connects to Cognos 8 BI and accesses the standard Welcome Page. Notice that at the top left corner, just below the Cognos 8 logo, you can see the "Log On" option.

1. Click on Cognos Connection

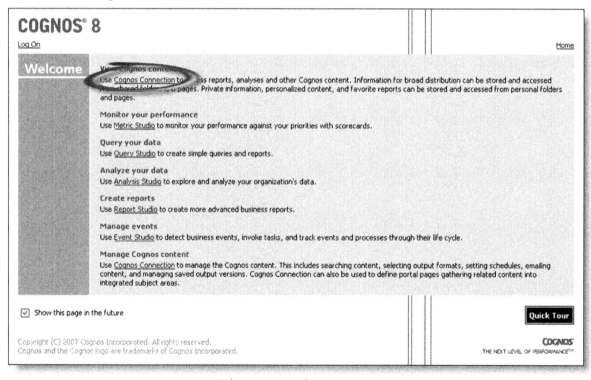

Welcome Page with Log On option

When we were not using security, we were working as an Anonymous user; you should now see your previous work when you choose Cognos Connection.

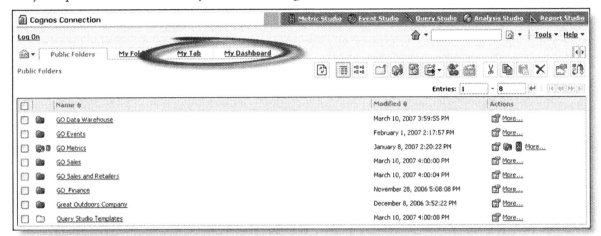

Cognos Connection for Anonymous user

For example, here you can see the two tabs we created in the previous chapter.

Let us see what happens when we activate security.

2. Click Log On from Cognos Connection (see link at top left under "Cognos Connection").

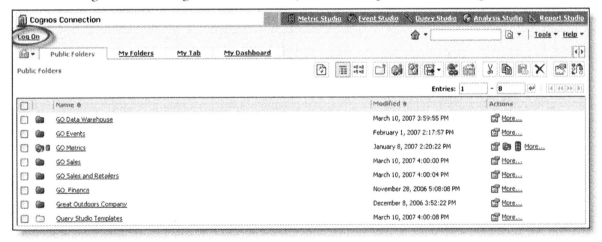

Log On as a registered user

An authentication page should appear that requests a user ID and password. Cognos 8 BI can be configured to use multiple authentication sources. As we configured our system (for the purposes of this tutorial) to have only one source, the Namespace (our name for the authentication source) is the only one, but you can get a list of all the available authentication sources in your organization from which to choose.

Authentication page

If you are not allowing Anonymous access to Cognos 8 BI in your installation, when you try to connect to Cognos, the Authentication page will be the first page you will see.

---

3. Enter your user ID and password. Press OK to authenticate.

Authenticating a user

We logged on with a user ID and password that we created in our MS Windows XP system, and we will use this user's access to demonstrate security. Once the user is authenticated, he or she will automatically be taken to the Welcome Page.

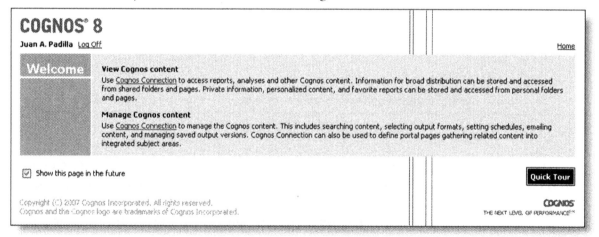

Authenticated user Welcome Page

Notice that the authenticated user Welcome Page lacks much of the functionality previously available to us as anonymous users. The reason for this is that this user is configured as a

Consumer and as such, does not have access to any of the Studios, and the system automatically configures itself accordingly.

4. Click on Cognos Connection.

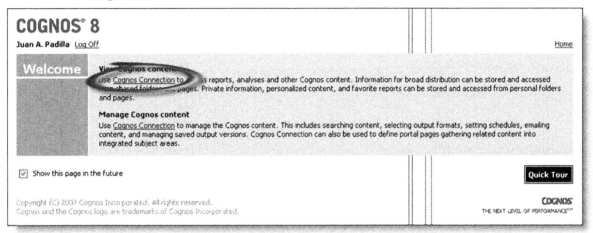

Getting into Cognos Connection authenticated

Roles can be modified to include more or fewer options, depending on business requirements, so your production environment may vary from what we present.

This should take you to the Cognos Connection interface. Notice that the information about the authenticated user is now displayed in the top left corner. Also notice that the Studios in the top right are missing, the user-defined tabs are not shown, and the toolbar in the Public Folders tab is missing some icons (mainly those regarding Metrics Studio). This is all a result of the restricted security for this Consumer user.

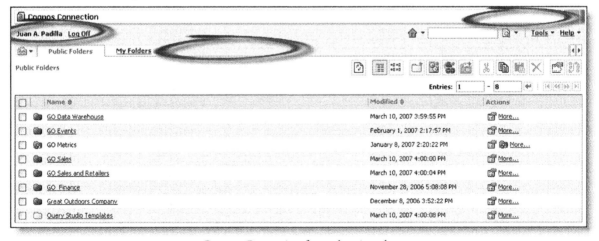

Cognos Connection for authenticated user

5. Navigate to the Report Studio Report Samples folder in the Great Outdoors Company package in Public Folders.

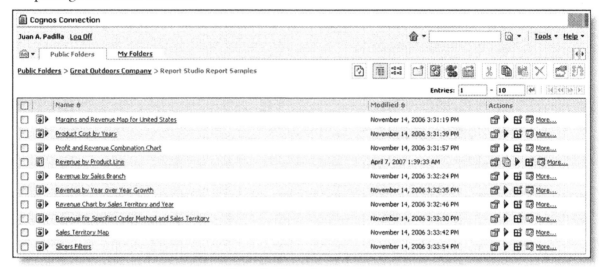

Entry list for authenticated user

Notice the missing options for opening the entry in a Studio. Since we, as Consumers, do not have access to Studios, the system automatically removes them from the list of available actions.

6. Expand the Tools menu.

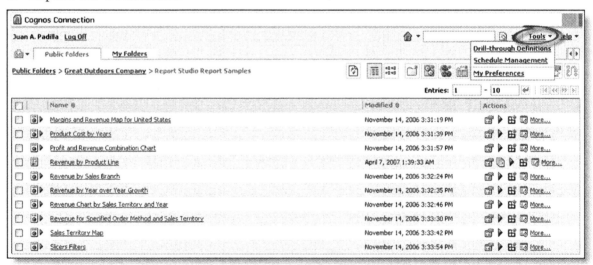

Tools for authenticated user

Notice also that only three options appear instead of the eight available for someone with a higher level of user access.

7. Click on My Folders.

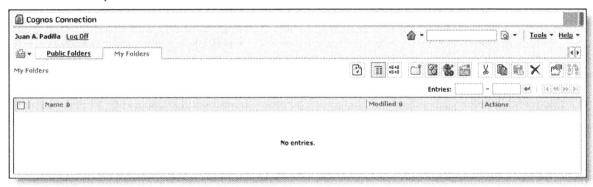

My Folders for authenticated user

Notice that My Folders is also empty. The content previously created in our tutorial belongs to the Anonymous user in his or her private My Folders. To share it with other users, "Anonymous" content will need to be moved to Public Folders and the appropriate permissions assigned.

Assigning permissions to objects

To simulate that we are assigning permissions to an owned object, let us create another sample folder.

1. Create a folder called New Sample Folder in My Folders.

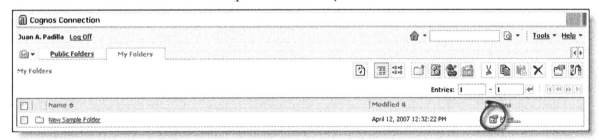

Created folder in My Folders

To assign access permission to an object, we have to modify its properties. Remember that the first property page of an object is General information, while the last page is Permissions.

2. Click on the Set Properties option in the available Actions for the newly created folder.

The first page contains General information about the object. Let us go to the last tab for security information.

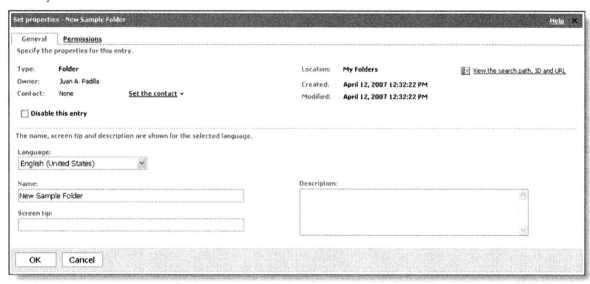

Set Properties - General information about the folder

3.   Click on the Permissions tab.

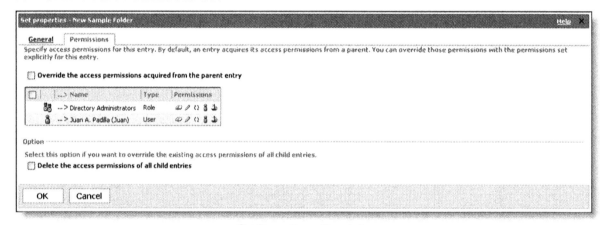

Set Properties – Permissions

Security in Cognos 8 BI is inherited, so the default permissions are those of the parent folder. To change the permissions for a specific folder, we have to set the Override option.

Security inheritance is quite useful, especially when deploying large numbers of BI objects. A good practice is to create a folder to organize objects by user needs and roles; this way, security can be set up at the folder level and all the objects in the folder inherit the permissions. Management of permissions can then be done via folders, making it much simpler all around.

---

4. Check the "Override the access permissions acquired from the parent entry" option to customize the permissions. Click on Add... to include additional users.

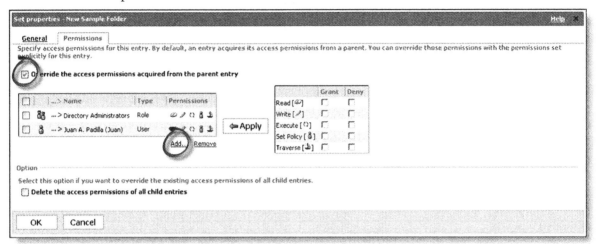

Override the permission inheritance

This should allow us to modify the permissions by adding and removing accesses.

Once you mark the Override option, the object will no longer inherit permissions from the parent. Any access modifications have to be performed manually and directly on the object, something that can become a management nightmare if the quantity of objects is considerable.

The page shows the available security namespaces. Namespaces are placeholders for the security objects created in Cognos or in external authentication systems. There will always be a Cognos namespace that contains system-reserved and other pre-defined entries, even when security is not set up and Anonymous access is enabled.

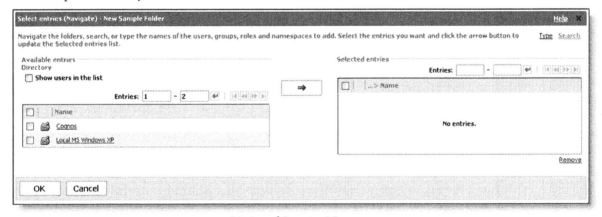

Listing of Security Namespaces

In a namespace, you will find definitions for one of three possible security objects:

User an actual account tied to authentication that can be used to connect to Cognos Connection. Users can not be defined within Cognos 8 BI itself, so external authentication sources have to be configured to provide Cognos 8 BI with users.

Role a specific function or responsibility that a user can perform in Cognos 8 BI, or in the organization that has access to some specific objects and/or capabilities.

Group a specific set of which a user is a member, where access is provided to specific objects and/or capabilities.

Understanding the security object User is usually quite straightforward. If you have a computer account on any system, this is probably where a User has been defined. In the case of Roles and Groups, it is not that simple because often these are both used interchangeably. Actually, in Cognos 8 BI, the distinction is mostly a matter of semantics.

In the Cognos pre-defined namespace, there are, by default, two sets of pre-defined security objects. These are:

- **System Reserved objects** - Pre-defined security objects that are built into the tool and are required for the proper system behavior. The system will not allow the deletion of any of the system objects.

  o **Anonymous** – This is a special system user, which is used when connecting to Cognos 8 BI without applying security. The administrator can disable this user, so no one can have access without proper authentication.

  o **All Authenticated Users** – This special system role includes any user that connects to the system by going through an authentication mechanism. Of course, this would exclude the Anonymous user.

  o **Everyone** – This special system role includes all users in the system, and includes both Anonymous and All Authenticated Users.

  o **System Administrator** – This special system role has access to all the system options.

- **Other Pre-defined objects** - Those objects included in the Cognos 8 BI installation as a default to jump-start the administration of a Cognos 8 BI installation, but which can be modified, and even removed, without major impact to the system. These include:

  o **Consumers** – Role permitting access to Cognos Connection for viewing and executing of BI objects.

  o **Query Users** - Role permitting access to Query Studio to create and maintain queries.

  o **Analysis Users** - Role permitting access to Analysis Studio to perform analysis.

  o **Metrics Users** - Role permitting access to Metrics Studio to monitor scorecards.

  o **Authors** - Role permitting access to Report Studio to create and maintain reports, and to Event Studio to create and maintain event agents.

  o **Metrics Authors** - Role permitting access to Metrics Studio to create and maintain scorecards.

o **Data Manager Authors** – Role permitting access to Data Manager, for managing and executing data loading procedures.

o **Directory Administrators** – Role to perform administrative tasks, such as managing security, defining database connections, distribution lists and setting printers.

o **Metrics Administrators** - Role to perform administrative tasks with Metrics Studio, such as loading a scorecard's current data and index recalculations.

o **Portal Administrators** - Role to perform administrative tasks in Cognos Connection, such as defining and applying portal styles.

o **Report Administrators** - Role to perform administrative tasks in Cognos Connection, such as monitoring and managing schedules and jobs.

o **Server Administrators** - Role to perform administrative tasks in Cognos Connection, such as managing, tuning and troubleshooting servers and services.

Although these are pre-defined by default, an administrator could have modified or deleted some of the Other Pre-Defined objects, or could have created new ones; thus, the list may look quite different if your organization is using a non-default installation.

Even in a default installation, there may be additional pre-defined roles for other Cognos products that we have not included in our series of Cognos 8 BI tools. Cognos has additional products for Software Development, Planning and Financial that are outside the scope of our tutorial.

---

5. Click on Local MS Windows XP to access the Users, Roles and Groups in our configured authentication source.

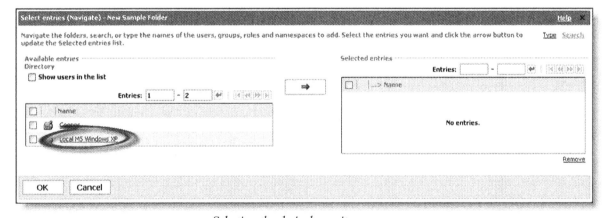

Selecting the desired security namespace

Cognos 8 BI will automatically connect to the authentication source and will transfer the security information for you to use in the permissions.

6. By default, only roles and groups are displayed. Click on "Show users in the list" to show users from the authentication source.

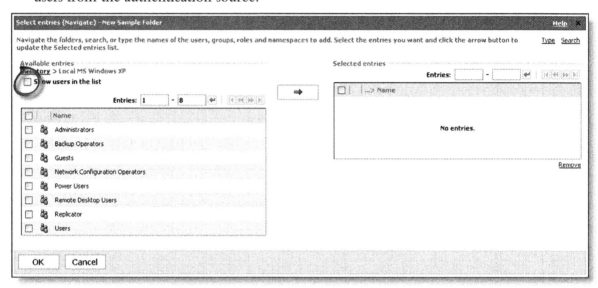

List of roles and groups from the authentication source

Now the listing should show roles, groups and users together. Let us give a user access to our New Sample Folder.

7. Click on Dorka M. Acosta and add her to the Selected entries list (by clicking the right arrow). Press OK.

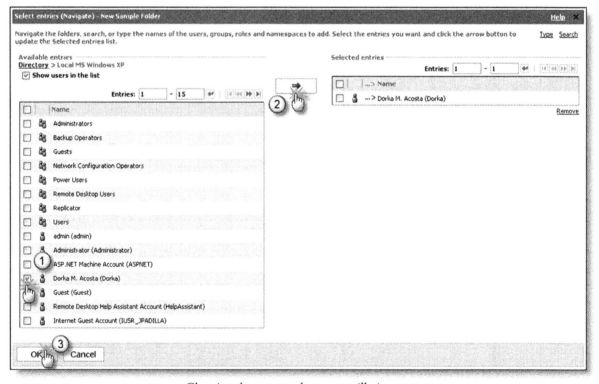

Choosing the user to whom you will give access

This adds the user to the access list for the folder. Now that we have added the user to the access list, we have to specify which permissions to assign.

8. Select Dorka M. Acosta, select the access (i.e., Read, Write, Execute, etc.) that we want to give to the user and click Apply to commit the selections.

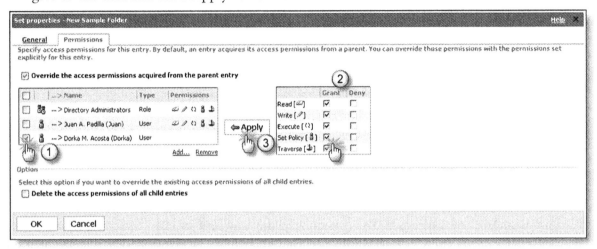

Assigning access to a user

It should now display the newly added user in the access list with the selected permissions.

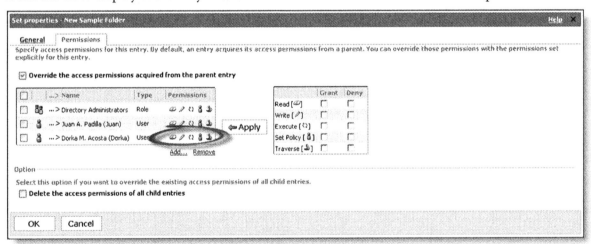

User with selected permissions

This is as far as we will go concerning security in this book, but you now have a good idea of how Cognos Connection will behave with security enabled.

Interesting Sample Reports

We have gone through the available functionality in Cognos Connection for Consumers. In the appendix, we have included some reports available in the sample demonstration data provided by Cognos, which show and expand functionality discussed throughout the book. For your benefit, we are including hints of the interesting options that make each report special.

Special thanks

This marks the end of the first book in the Cognos 8 BI series and introduces the basic infrastructure of Cognos 8 BI, particularly the standard portal Cognos Connection. Future books in the series will tackle some of the advanced features of Cognos 8 BI in much more detail.

I thank you for your interest in Cognos 8 BI, and hope you have enjoyed this book and found it useful. Please contact me via my website at **www.cognosbooks.com** or via email at **jpadilla@cognosbooks.com**.

Appendix A: Exploring Sample Reports

Cognos 8 BI includes a wealth of sample reports in the demonstration databases and packages. To allow you to discover for yourself the additional functionality available to Cognos 8 BI, we have listed the most appealing sample reports as well as what makes them so interesting.

GO Data Warehouse

Reports available through the GO Data Warehouse package.

Reports Included

The following reports within the GO Data Warehouse package contain features of interest:

- Employee Profile
- Sales Target by Region
- Tool Tips

Report Name: Employee Profile

Cognos report description

"Human resources report showing data for each employee."

What is interesting about this report?

- The use of a complex Search and Select prompt, which allows you to execute a search based on complex criteria and then select the desired options from a list of matching results. You can choose from a menu of options that will make the search criteria quite powerful and specific to your needs.

Complex prompts are standard in Cognos 8 BI; a Professional Author can create a report and easily include powerful prompts to enhance the report utility.

- The use of an embedded prompt in the actual report, with a drop-down list that permits you to execute the report for other Employees without having to get out of the report and start over.

Location

In folder: Public Folders > Go Data Warehouse

Parameter Page

The first page is a customized prompt page that contains a Select and Search prompt.

First Page

The first report page shows the standard cover page of the demos. Reports can include a standard cover page to show relevant report information, such as the report name, the date/time and user that executed, parameters and other information.

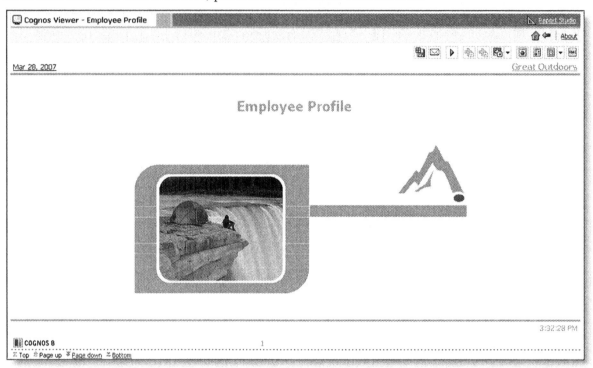

Report Pages

This report shows an employee profile with sales contribution. It also displays a prompt that allows you to execute the report for another employee.

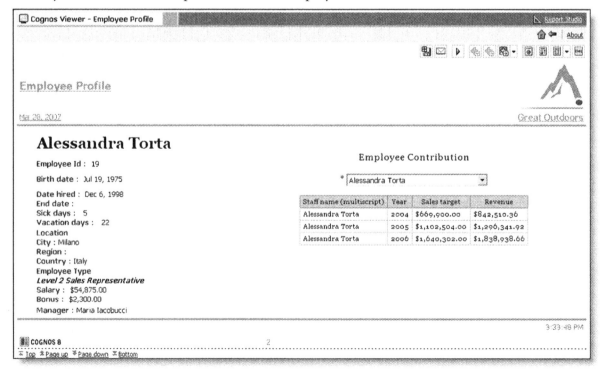

Report Name: Sales Target by Region

Cognos report description

"Report showing sales target by region, using a prompt to provide values for the report."

What is interesting about this report?

- The use of a drop-down list to filter the report data.

- The use of multiple objects in the same report: a grouped list and a 100% stacked column chart. That chart shows the columns as percentages of a whole (similar to a pie chart), instead of actual values.

Location

In folder: Public Folders > Go Data Warehouse

Parameter Page

The first page is a customized prompt page with a Value prompt (the drop-down list).

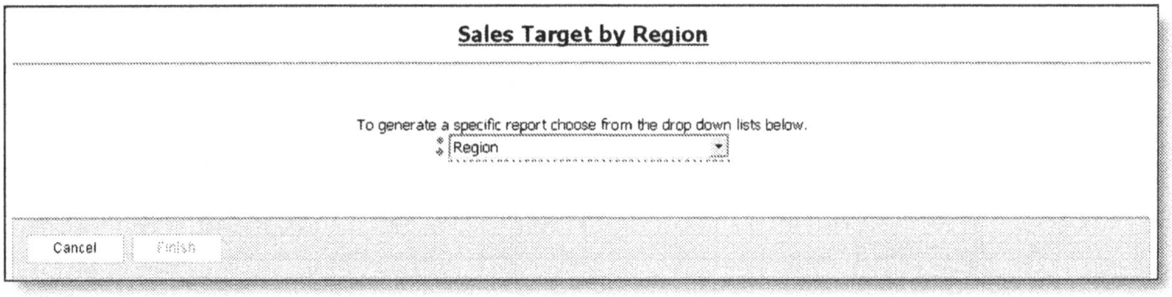

Sales Target by Region

To generate a specific report choose from the drop down lists below.

Region

Cancel   Finish

Report Pages

This report shows different Sales Regions with Position and Sales People, including their Sales Targets.   Notice how the report highlights information for Sales Targets of more than $1M.

The last page also shows how you can include additional objects, in this case a Chart, in the same report.

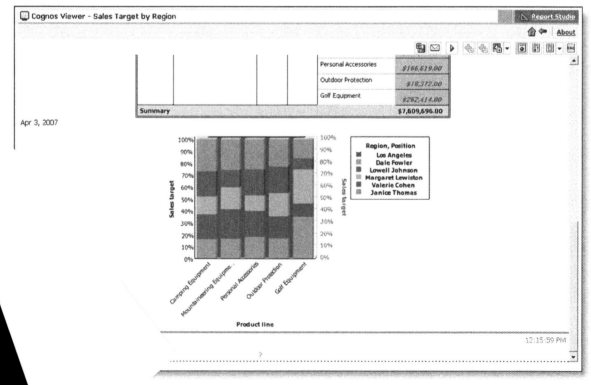

Report Name: Tool Tips

Cognos report description

"Report that shows tool tips and baselines in chart."

What is interesting about this report?

- The use of a drop-down list to filter the report data.

- The use of tool tips to provide details of data in the report.

- The use of chart objects, such as Bubble Chart and Radar Chart. The Bubble Chart allows you to plot a value against two axes and you can use the size of the bubble to act as another value. In the Radar Chart, you can plot one value across multiple axes.

Location

In folder: Public Folders > Go Data Warehouse

Report Pages

The chart shows the relation between Revenue and Quantity for Product Lines, with the size of the bubble showing the Gross Margin of each product line.

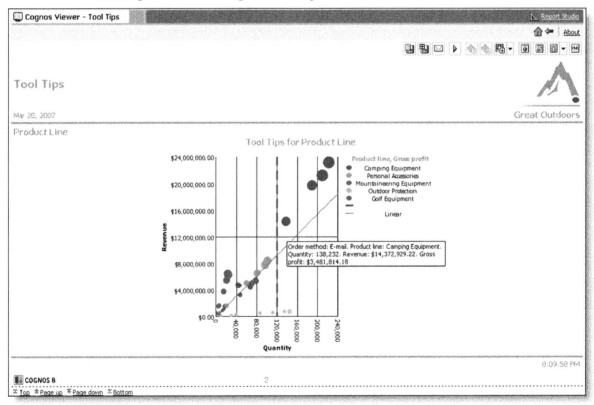

The last page also shows a complex radar chart plotting multiple values at the same time.

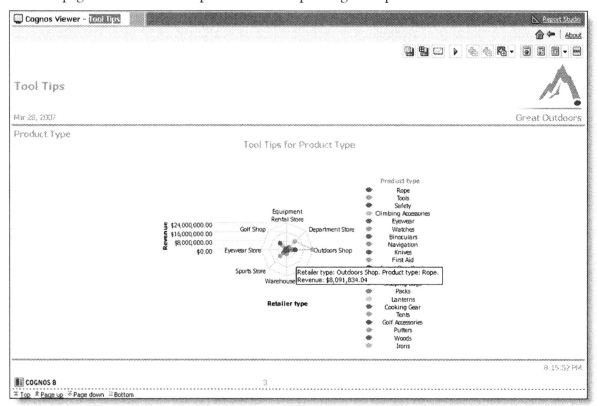

GO Sales and Retailers

Reports available through the GO Sales and Retailers package.

Reports Included

The following reports within the GO Sales and Retailers package contain features of interest:

- Actual Sales against Target Sales
- Actual Sales against Target Sales-burst
- Banded Report
- Basket Analysis with Total Contribution (Top 10 Rank)
- Business Details Drill Through
- Consumer Trends
- Cost of Goods
- Custom Grouping
- Customer Invoice
- Global Sales
- Global Sales (1)
- GO Business View
- GO Media
- Mailing Labels
- Margin Cost and Volume Report
- Multi-Grain Fact
- Multiple Charts
- Order Analysis
- Percent contribution by country
- Product Comparison Charts
- Product Line by Year
- Product Line by Year-prompt
- Product Revenue – Lifetime_Q2
- Product Summary
- Products ranked by Revenue
- Report with totals
- Retailer Contact

- Retailer Contact (Multiple Prompt Values)
- Sales Representative Contact List
- Union Crosstab
- Waterfall Chart

Report Name: Actual Sales against Target Sales

Cognos report description

"The report shows a simple list with conditional formatting that drills through to the Sales Representative Contact List report."

What is interesting about this report?

- The use of drill through reports.   The staff name is a hyperlink that will automatically take you to another report while filtering for the selected staff name.

- The use of conditional formatting.   The column named difference is actually color coded to highlight exceptional values.

Location

In folder: Public Folders > GO Sales and Retailers > Report Studio Report Samples

Report Pages

The report shows staff names with their corresponding sales and targets.   It highlights when the revenue is below the targets.   It also provides access to additional details regarding the Staff Name by using a hyperlink tied to specific values.

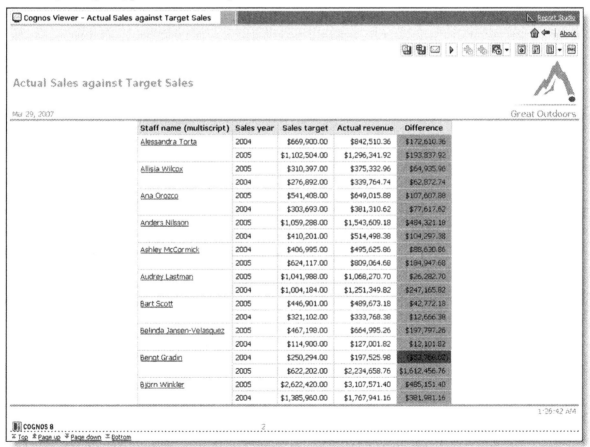

Report Name: Actual Sales against Target Sales-burst

Cognos report description

"Report that is set up for bursting to email addresses.   The email addresses point to sales representatives in the Sales reps table in the GOSALES database."

What is interesting about this report?

This is the same report as Actual Sales against Target Sales report, but it has been configured for bursting, so a Professional Author can explore the setup required for bursting.

Location

In folder: Public Folders > GO Sales and Retailers > Report Studio Report Samples

Report Name: Banded Report

Cognos report description

"Banded report that shows Product name, Quantity and Revenue with sales opportunities for each Product line category."

What is interesting about this report?

- Its use of a customized format for the list. By default, a list in Cognos 8 BI summarizes data at the *end* of each group. In this case, we can see the totals at the *beginning* of the groups.

Location

In folder: Public Folders > GO Sales and Retailers > Report Studio Report Samples

Report Pages

The report shows sales information (quantity and revenue) in a customized format by presenting the totals at the top instead of the more commonly used totals at the bottom.

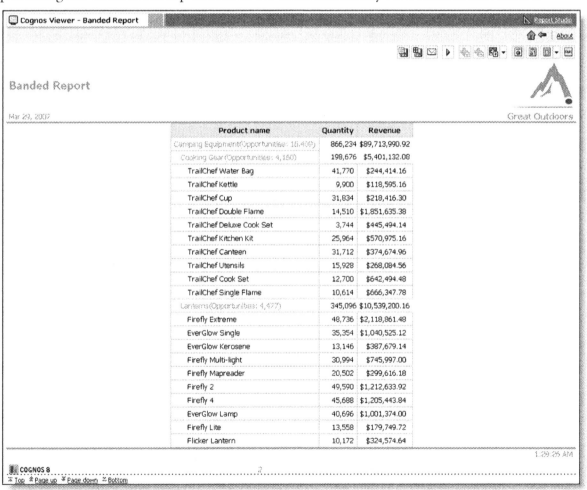

Report Name: Basket Analysis with Total Contribution (Top 10 Rank)

Cognos report description

"Pairing analysis report that uses prompts to compare two products. Orders are totaled and ranked, and the top ten orders are shown."

What is interesting about this report?

- The use of two side-by-side drop-down lists prompts for product names to compare them in a report. The report analyzes the sales of two different products, when sold in the same order. This can be used to create bundles of products and/or promotions.

Location

In folder: Public Folders > GO Sales and Retailers > Report Studio Report Samples

Parameter Page

The first page is a customized prompt page with two drop down list prompts.

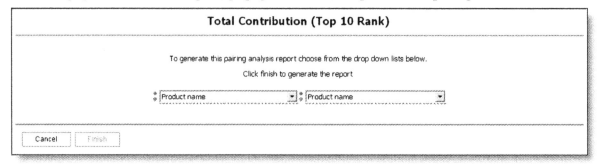

Report Pages

The report shows data from two different products to analyze pairing tendencies.

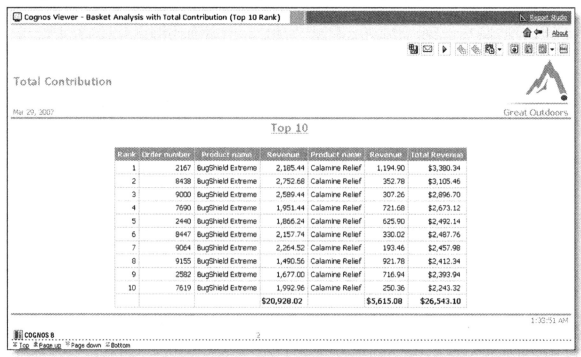

Report Name: Business Details Drill Through

Cognos report description

"Report that shows product details in charts. This report is a drill-through target report for the GO Business View report. You can also run it as a product-prompted report."

What is interesting about this report?

- Its use of multiple report objects in the same report page. This report serves as a detail report to which other reports drill through.

Location

In folder: Public Folders > GO Sales and Retailers > Report Studio Report Samples

Report Pages

The report shows an interesting overview about a specific Product Type. This report is used as a detailed drill-through report that is accessed by using hyperlinks in other summarized reports.

Report Name: Consumer Trends

Cognos report description

"This complex report shows a list chart, bar chart and product images to illustrate revenue by product type."

What is interesting about this report?

- The use of two side-by-side drop-down list prompts.

- The use of multiple report objects in the same report page.

- The use of an embedded prompt in the actual report. A drop-down list allows you to execute the report for other products without having to get out of the report.

- The use of context sensitive images related to the product being evaluated.

Location

In folder: Public Folders > GO Sales and Retailers > Report Studio Report Samples

Parameter Page

The first page is a customized prompt page with two independent Value prompts (drop-down lists).

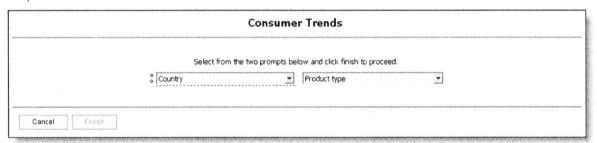

Report Pages

The report shows filtered information based on the prompt values. It includes a chart, a list and related images. It also allows you to execute the report dynamically for other products by using the embedded prompt.

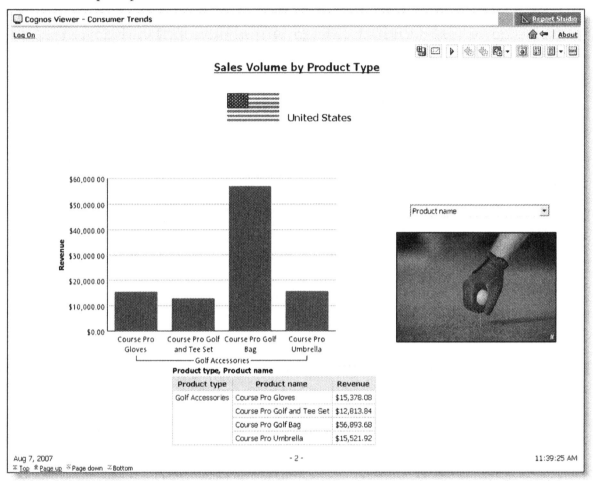

Report Name: Cost of Goods

Cognos report description

"Illustrates conditional formatting on a crosstab report."

What is interesting about this report?

- The use of a complex crosstab structure. Crosstabs are similar to MS Excel spreadsheets because they show the information in rows and columns.

- The use of conditional formatting. The column named Gross Profit Margin is actually color-coded to highlight exceptional values.

Location

In folder: Public Folders > GO Sales and Retailers > Report Studio Report Samples

Report Pages

The report shows a complex crosstab with highlighted data.

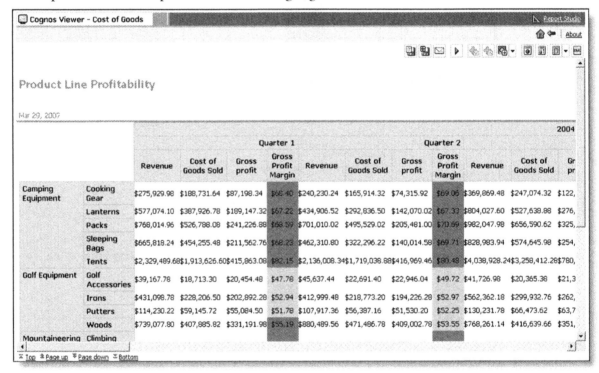

Report Name: Custom Grouping

Cognos report description

"Report showing the ability to group products with conditional statements. For example, show all products that start with the letter S."

What is interesting about this report?

- The use of a custom grouping mechanism to provide better cluster analysis.

Location

In folder: Public Folders > GO Sales and Retailers > Report Studio Report Samples

Report Pages

The report shows a list report with custom groupings.

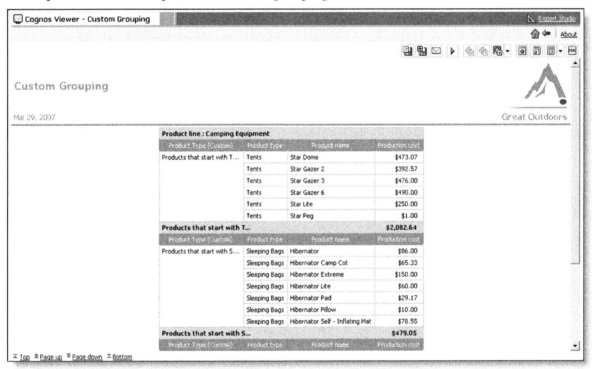

Report Name: Customer Invoice

Cognos report description

"The report illustrates The Great Outdoors Company invoice statement."

What is interesting about this report?

- It provides a sample of a highly structured and formatted report.

Location

In folder: Public Folders > GO Sales and Retailers > Report Studio Report Samples

Report Pages

The report shows a highly formatted invoice created using the Cognos 8 BI authoring tools.

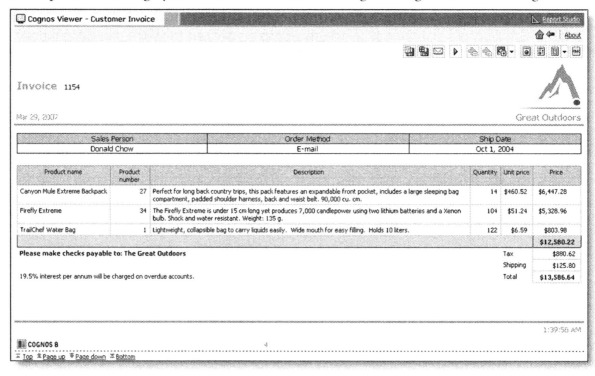

Report Name: Global Sales

Cognos report description

"This book style report uses multiple pages and charts to show global sales results."

What is interesting about this report?

- It shows charts, lists and crosstabs together in the same report.

Location

In folder: Public Folders > GO Sales and Retailers > Report Studio Report Samples

Report Pages

The report shows a chart and a related list on the same page.

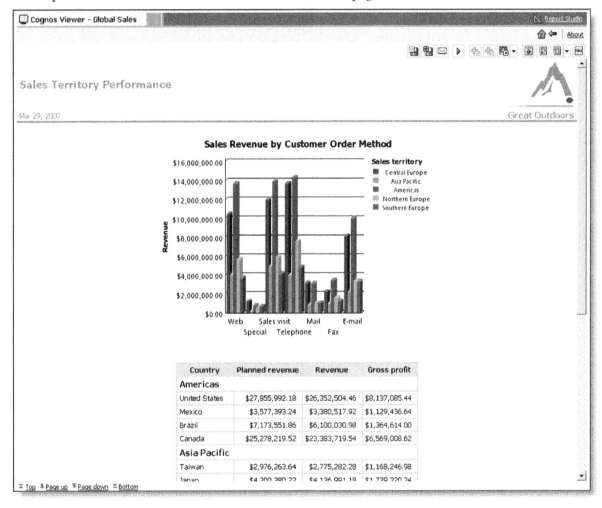

By browsing the report within several more pages, you will see another chart.

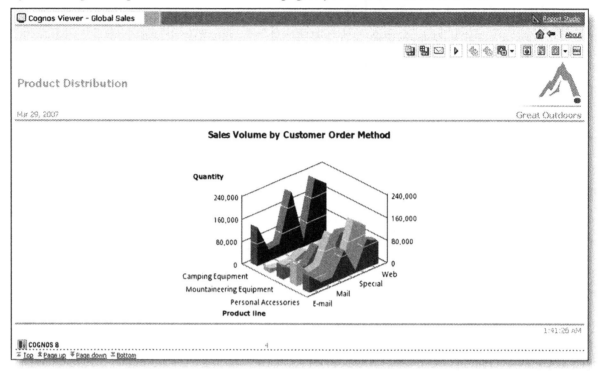

Further, you will find a complex crosstab. All of these objects are in the same report.

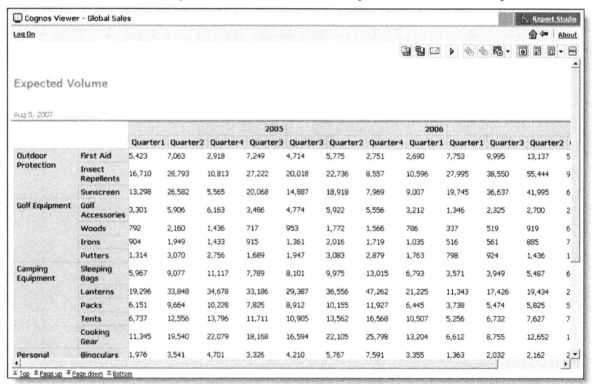

Report Name: Global Sales (1)

Cognos report description

"The report is a cut-down version of the Global Sales report."

What is interesting about this report?

- It shows charts and crosstabs together in the same report.

Location

In folder: Public Folders > GO Sales and Retailers > Report Studio Report Samples

Report Pages

The report shows a complex crosstab...

Cognos Viewer - Global Sales (1)												Report Studio

Expected Volume

Mar 29, 2007

		2005				2006				2004		
		Quarter 1	Quarter 2	Quarter 4	Quarter 3	Quarter 3	Quarter 2	Quarter 4	Quarter 1	Quarter 1	Quarter 3	Quar
Outdoor Protection	First Aid	5,423	7,063	2,918	7,249	4,714	5,775	2,751	2,690	7,753	9,995	13,137
	Insect Repellents	16,710	28,793	10,813	27,222	20,018	22,736	8,557	10,596	27,995	38,550	55,444
	Sunscreen	13,298	26,582	5,565	20,068	14,887	18,918	7,969	9,007	19,745	36,637	41,995
Golf Equipment	Golf Accessories	3,301	5,906	6,163	3,486	4,774	5,922	5,556	3,212	1,346	2,325	2,700
	Woods	792	2,160	1,436	717	953	1,772	1,566	786	337	519	919
	Irons	904	1,949	1,433	915	1,361	2,016	1,719	1,035	516	561	885
	Putters	1,314	3,070	2,756	1,689	1,947	3,083	2,879	1,763	798	924	1,436
Camping Equipment	Sleeping Bags	5,967	9,077	11,117	7,789	8,101	9,975	13,015	6,793	3,571	3,949	5,487
	Lanterns	19,296	33,848	34,678	33,186	29,387	36,556	47,262	21,225	11,343	17,426	19,434
	Packs	6,151	9,664	10,228	7,825	8,912	10,155	11,927	6,445	3,738	5,474	5,825
	Tents	6,737	12,556	13,796	11,711	10,905	13,562	16,568	10,507	5,256	6,732	7,627
	Cooking Gear	11,345	19,540	22,079	18,168	16,594	22,105	25,798	13,204	6,612	8,755	12,652
Personal Accessories	Binoculars	1,976	3,541	4,701	3,326	4,210	5,767	7,591	3,355	1,363	2,032	2,162
	Navigation	3,525	5,870	6,463	4,010	4,654	6,523	9,704	4,198	1,968	2,478	3,452
	Eyewear	2,928	6,075	5,043	4,601	5,505	6,508	6,409	4,098	2,517	2,858	3,328
	Watches	5,323	9,557	10,855	9,671	11,981	12,201	13,609	5,913	3,051	6,660	5,315
	Knives	6,073	12,813	14,818	12,337	12,451	17,185	20,246	8,860	4,708	7,568	8,463
Mountaineering Equipment	Rope	2,929	6,004	5,066	3,813	4,360	6,356	6,391	3,219			
	Climbing Accessories	9,409	20,018	18,239	13,937	15,615	20,902	24,380	9,845			
	Safety	1,274	3,361	2,803	2,084	2,672	3,237	3,506	1,565			

Top Page up Page down Bottom

followed by a chart.

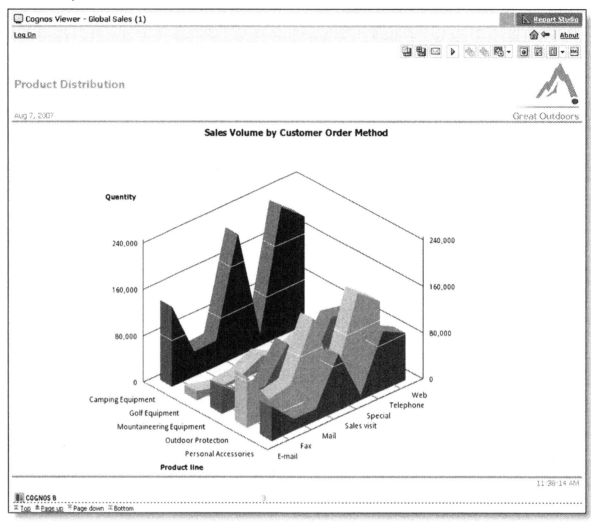

Report Name: GO Business View

Cognos report description

"Two-page business report showing a combination of metrics across the Great Outdoors company. Multiple charting types are used."

What is interesting about this report?

- In two pages, it includes a wealth of charts and lists.

- The use of drill-through reports. Underline fields are hyperlinks that will take you to another report, automatically filtering for the selected product.

Location

In folder: Public Folders > GO Sales and Retailers > Report Studio Report Samples

Report Pages

The report shows multiple charts and lists related to a specific Product Line.

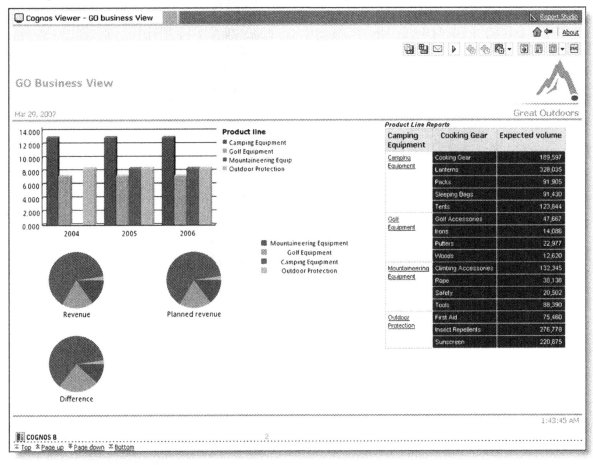

These are followed by additional charts and lists related to the Product Line.

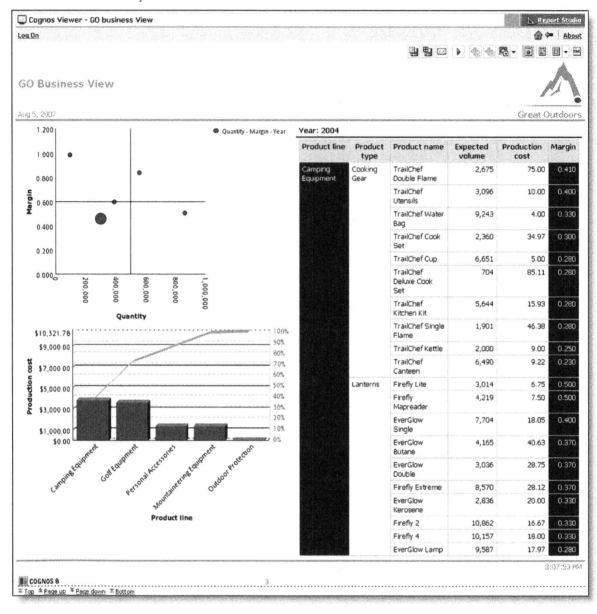

Report Name: GO Media

Cognos report description

"The report uses a media file in combination with multiple charting styles."

What is interesting about this report?

- The use of a drop-down list prompt.

- Its use of multiple report objects in the same report page, including a video object.

- Its use of an embedded prompt in the actual report. A drop-down list allows you to execute the report for other products without having to get out of the report.

- The use of context sensitive images related to the product being evaluated.

Location

In folder: Public Folders > GO Sales and Retailers > Report Studio Report Samples

Report Pages

The report shows charts, lists, images and videos related to a specific Product Name. The embedded prompt can be used to execute the report dynamically.

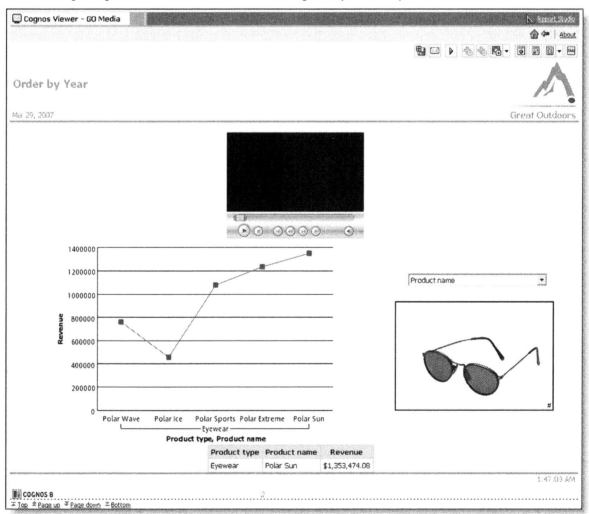

Report Name: Mailing Labels

Cognos report description

"This template style report illustrates a Multilingual mailing list for retailers of the Great Outdoors company."

What is interesting about this report?

- The use of a report to generate mailing labels.

Location

In folder: Public Folders > GO Sales and Retailers > Report Studio Report Samples

Report Pages

The report shows how to create mailing labels as a report.

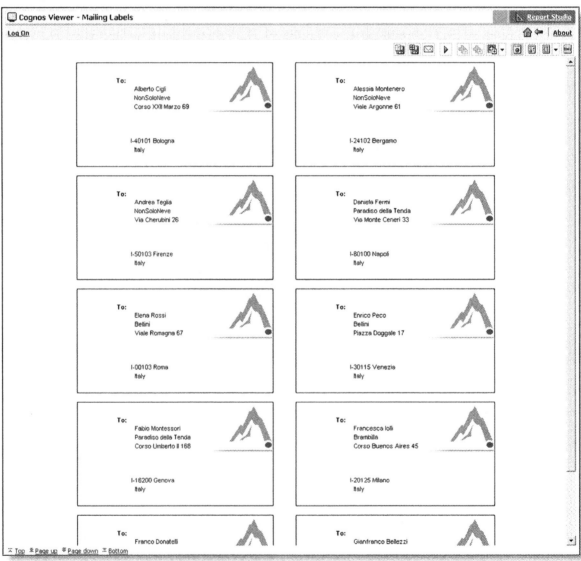

Report Name: Margin Cost and Volume Report

Cognos report description

"Report showing volume and production costs using various chart types. The report drills through on Product line."

What is interesting about this report?

- Complex layout with crosstab, charts and lists.
- The use of drill through reports. Underlined fields are hyperlinks that will automatically take you to another report filtering for the selected product.

Location

In folder: Public Folders > GO Sales and Retailers > Report Studio Report Samples

Report Pages

The report shows an impressive amount of information about margin, cost and volume.

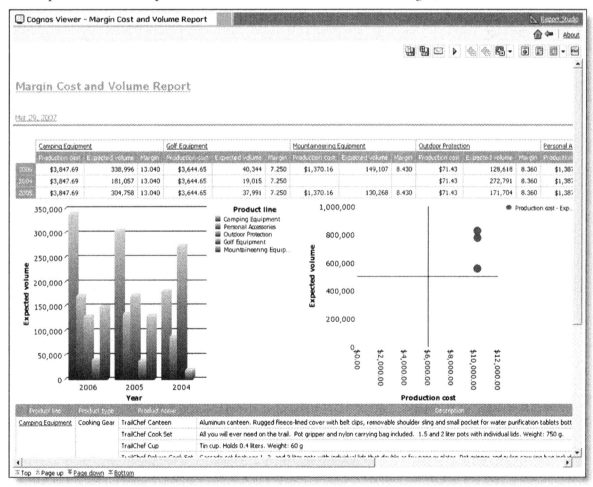

Report Name: Multi-Grain Fact

Cognos report description

"Report that reads two fact tables, each at different levels of granularity, and combines them. Bookmarks are used to permit easy navigation within the report."

What is interesting about this report?

- Internally combines multiple queries into a single report.
- Use the concept of bookmarks used in HTML pages to easily navigate from the table of content to specific areas in the document and back.

Location

In folder: Public Folders > GO Sales and Retailers > Report Studio Report Samples

Report Pages

The report shows a Table of Contents at the top. This Table of Contents can be used to navigate to specific areas of the report. Near the middle of the report, you can see an option called "TOP". Selecting that option will bring you back to the Table of Contents from any report page.

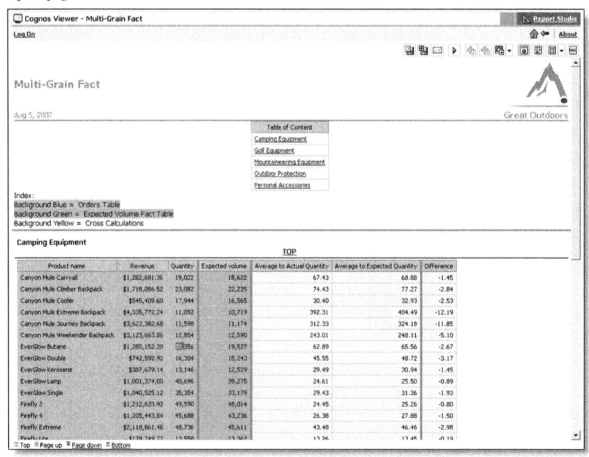

Report Name: Multiple Charts

Cognos report description

"Report showing similar information on one page using multiple chart types.   Visual representation of metrics."

What is interesting about this report?

- Use of multiple report objects in the same report page.

Location

In folder: Public Folders > GO Sales and Retailers > Report Studio Report Samples

Report Pages

The report shows a complex layout with multiple objects.

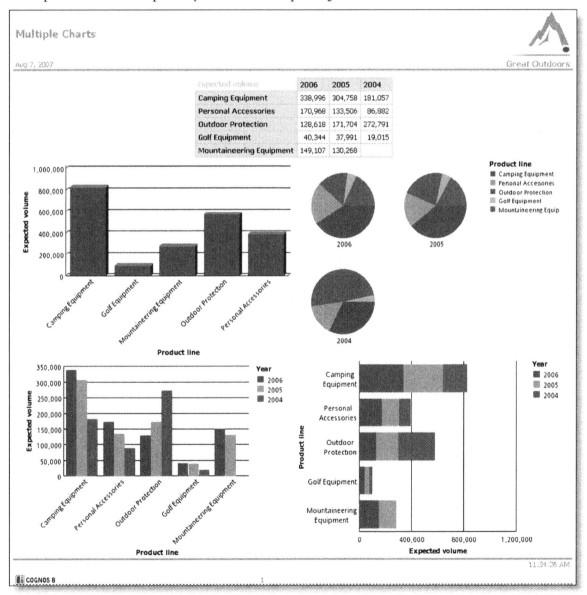

Report Name: Order Analysis

Cognos report description

"Pairing analysis report that prompts the user for two products, and shows the orders that they both appear in."

What is interesting about this report?

- The use of two side-by-side list prompts.

Location

In folder: Public Folders > GO Sales and Retailers > Report Studio Report Samples

Parameter Page

The first page is a customized prompt page with two prompts.

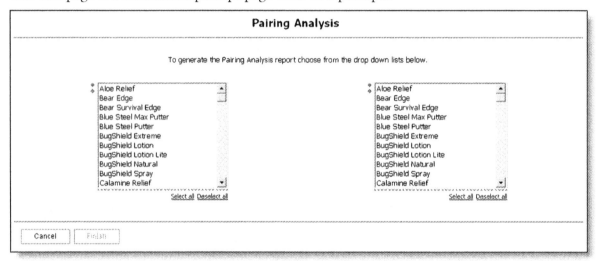

Report Pages

The report shows the top orders containing both products.

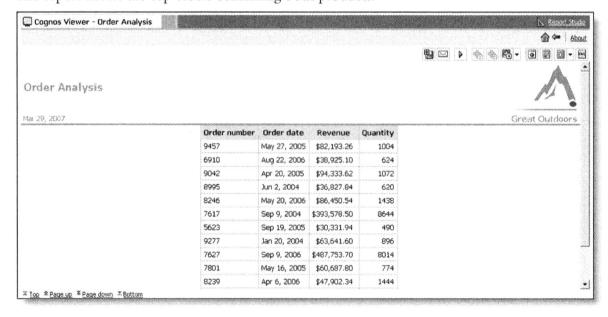

Report Name: Percent contribution by country

Cognos report description

"Report showing the percentage of products sold by country as well as a percentage comparison across other countries. Bookmarks are used for easy navigation throughout the report."

What is interesting about this report?

- The use of a complex prompt.   It uses a Date Prompt to select multiple date ranges.

- The use of the concept of bookmarks used in HTML pages to easily navigate from the table of contents to specific areas in the document and back.

Location

In folder: Public Folders > GO Sales and Retailers > Report Studio Report Samples

Parameter Page

The first page is a customized prompt page with a Date prompt.

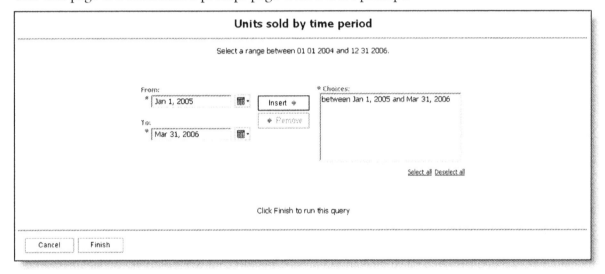

Report Pages

The report shows a Table of Contents using countries as hyperlinks to detailed data.

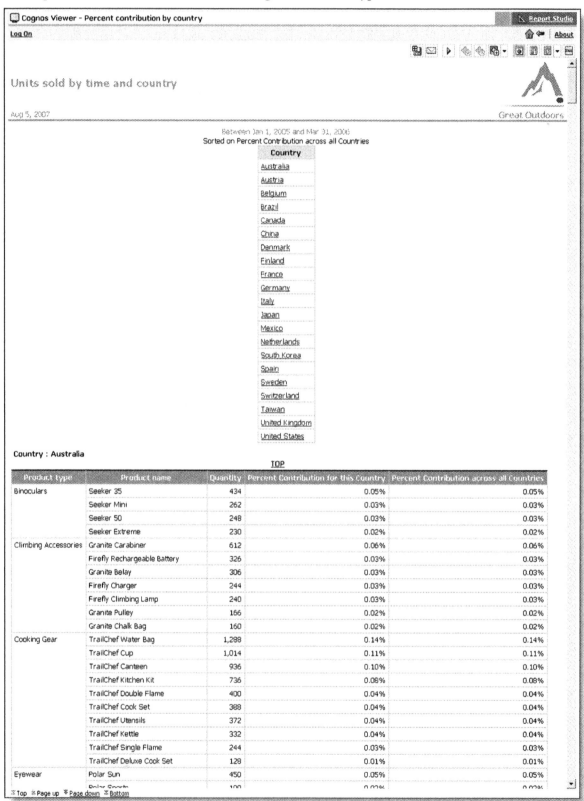

Report Name: Product Comparison Charts

Cognos report description

"The report uses multiple charts to reveal trends and relationships that are not evident in tabular reports."

What is interesting about this report?

- The use of multiple chart objects in the same report page.

Location

In folder: Public Folders > GO Sales and Retailers > Report Studio Report Samples

Report Pages

The report shows multiple charts on the same page.

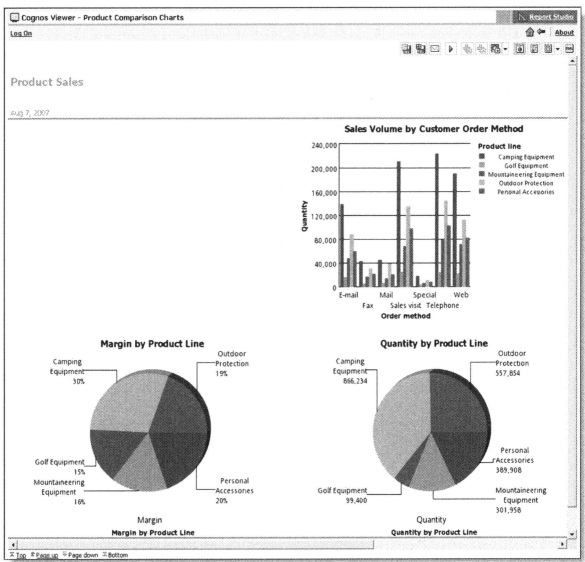

Report Name: Product Line by Year

Cognos report description

"This is a nested line chart."

What is interesting about this report?

- The use of multi-line charts to analyze trends.

Location

In folder: Public Folders > GO Sales and Retailers > Report Studio Report Samples

Report Pages

The report shows a multi-line chart used to visualize trends.

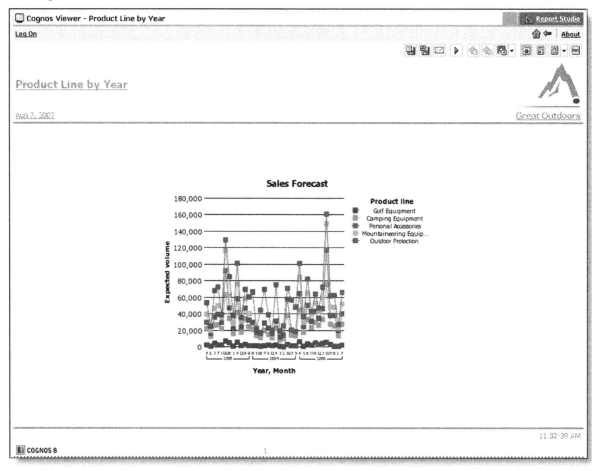

Report Name: Product Line by Year-prompt

Cognos report description

"The report illustrates the use of adding a prompt to an existing report."

What is interesting about this report?

- The use of multi-line charts to analyze trends.
- The use of embedded prompts in the actual report. They add interactivity to the report.

Location

In folder: Public Folders > GO Sales and Retailers > Report Studio Report Samples

Report Pages

The report shows a multi-line chart used to visualize trends, but it also includes embedded prompts for dynamic execution with other options.

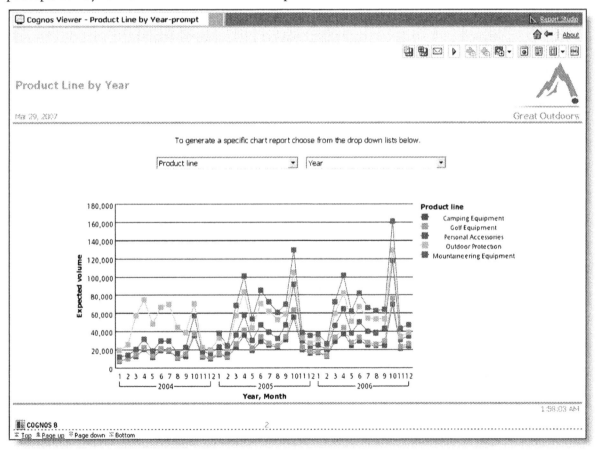

Report Name: Product Revenue – Lifetime_Q2

Cognos report description

"Pairing analysis report showing lifetime revenue for each product with sales from Q2 in 2002."

What is interesting about this report?

- The calculation of two different totals in the same query.

Location

In folder: Public Folders > GO Sales and Retailers > Report Studio Report Samples

Report Pages

The report shows revenue for products for a specific quarter and lifetime.

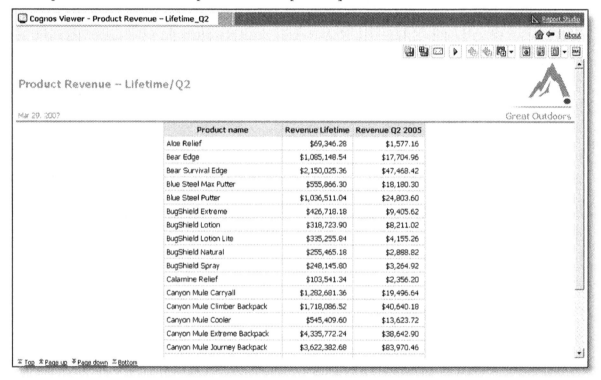

The report table shown in the image:

Product name	Revenue Lifetime	Revenue Q2 2005
Aloe Relief	$69,346.28	$1,577.16
Bear Edge	$1,085,148.54	$17,704.96
Bear Survival Edge	$2,150,025.36	$47,468.42
Blue Steel Max Putter	$555,866.30	$18,180.30
Blue Steel Putter	$1,036,511.04	$24,803.60
BugShield Extreme	$426,718.18	$9,405.62
BugShield Lotion	$318,723.90	$8,211.02
BugShield Lotion Lite	$335,255.84	$4,155.26
BugShield Natural	$255,465.18	$2,888.82
BugShield Spray	$248,145.80	$3,264.92
Calamine Relief	$103,541.34	$2,356.20
Canyon Mule Carryall	$1,282,681.36	$19,496.64
Canyon Mule Climber Backpack	$1,718,086.52	$40,640.18
Canyon Mule Cooler	$545,409.60	$13,623.72
Canyon Mule Extreme Backpack	$4,335,772.24	$38,642.90
Canyon Mule Journey Backpack	$3,622,382.68	$83,970.46

Report Name: Product Summary

Cognos report description

"The report uses a prompt page to query a list report."

What is interesting about this report?

- The use of two side-by-side drop-down lists prompts in cascade mode. Cascade mode means that the values of the second prompt are restricted to those of the first.

- The use of context sensitive images related to the product being displayed.

Location

In folder: Public Folders > GO Sales and Retailers > Report Studio Report Samples

Parameter Page

The first page is a customized prompt page with two prompts. The prompts are configured in cascade mode, where one depends on the other.

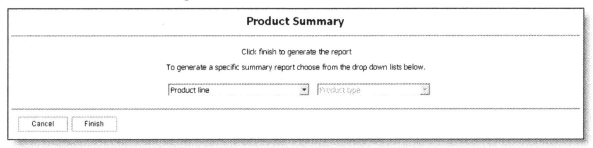

Report Pages

The report shows detailed product data, including images.

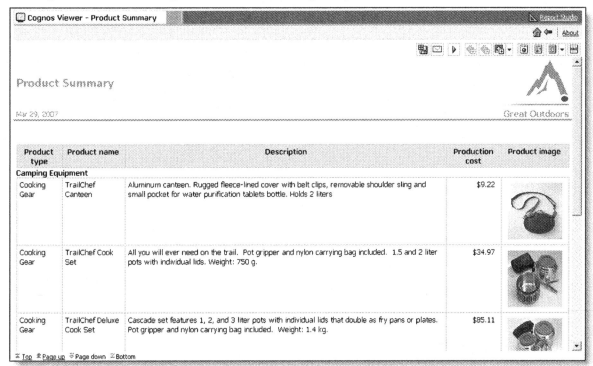

Report Name: Products ranked by Revenue

Cognos report description

"Pairing analysis report that prompts the user to select a product, order year, and revenue. The results are ranked by revenue."

What is interesting about this report?

- The use of a prompt page with multiple parameters.
- The use of a ranking function and filter.

Location

In folder: Public Folders > GO Sales and Retailers > Report Studio Report Samples

Parameter Page

The first page is a customized prompt page with multiple prompts, including informational messages.

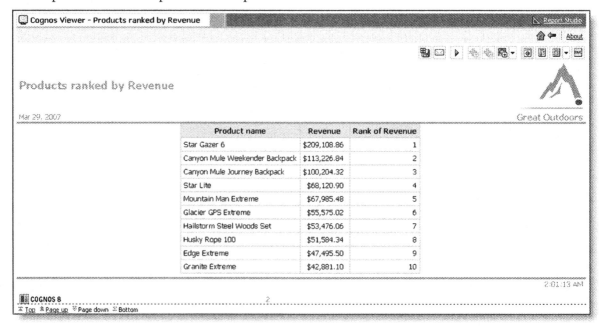

Report Pages

The report shows the top 10 revenue producers.

Product name	Revenue	Rank of Revenue
Star Gazer 6	$209,108.86	1
Canyon Mule Weekender Backpack	$113,226.84	2
Canyon Mule Journey Backpack	$100,204.32	3
Star Lite	$68,120.90	4
Mountain Man Extreme	$67,985.48	5
Glacier GPS Extreme	$55,575.02	6
Hailstorm Steel Woods Set	$53,476.06	7
Husky Rope 100	$51,584.34	8
Edge Extreme	$47,495.50	9
Granite Extreme	$42,881.10	10

Report Name: Report with totals

Cognos report description

"List report that uses prompts to show product sales by date and product value lifetime contribution."

What is interesting about this report?

- The use of a complex prompt. It uses a Date Prompt to visually select a date from a calendar.

Location

In folder: Public Folders > GO Sales and Retailers > Report Studio Report Samples

Parameter Page

The first page is a customized prompt page with both a Date prompt and a Text prompt.

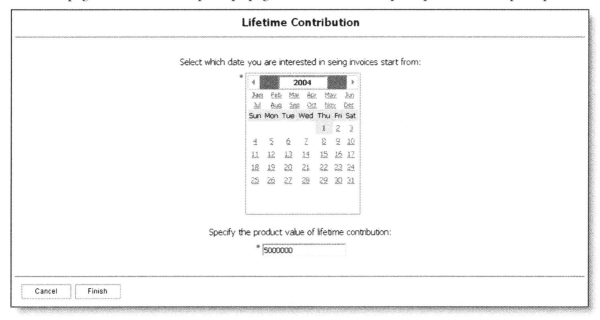

Report Name: Retailer Contact

Cognos report description

"A list report that uses a prompt page. It is also used as a drill through report."

What is interesting about this report?

- This report is used as a drill-through report for other reports. If you run the report standalone, i.e. choosing it from Cognos Connection, it will display a prompt asking for a Retailer Name. When it is used as a drill-through report, the value is passed automatically from one report to the other, so the prompt is not displayed.

Location

In folder: Public Folders > GO Sales and Retailers > Report Studio Report Samples

Parameter Page

The first page is a customized prompt page with a Value prompt (drop-down list).

Report Pages

The report shows filtered data by retailer.

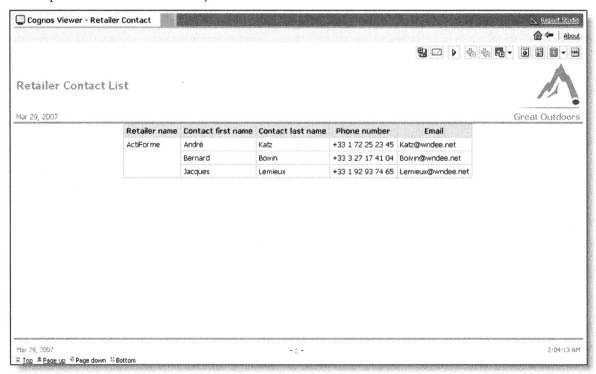

Report Name: Retailer Contact (Multiple Prompt Values)

Cognos report description

"This list report accepts multiple prompt values. It is referenced by the Event Studio User Guide and the Event Studio Quick Tour."

What is interesting about this report?

- This report is the same as the previous one, but this time with a prompt that allows you to select multiple Retailer Names.

Location

In folder: Public Folders > GO Sales and Retailers > Report Studio Report Samples

Parameter Page

The first page is a customized prompt page with a multi-value prompt.

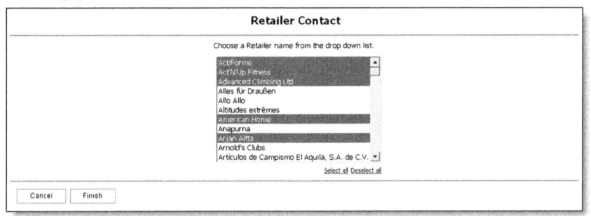

Report Pages

The report shows filtered data by multiple retailers.

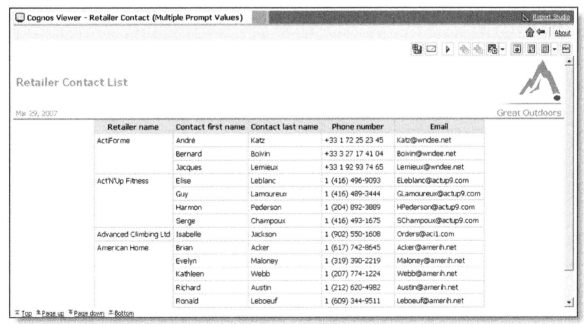

Report Name: Sales Representative Contact List

Cognos report description

"The report illustrates multiple prompt styles on the same report page. It is also used as a drill through report."

What is interesting about this report?

- The use of multi-select lists as prompts in the report body.

Location

In folder: Public Folders > GO Sales and Retailers > Report Studio Report Samples

Report Pages

The report shows the contact information for sales representatives. It also includes embedded prompts that allow you to select sales representatives and show their information.

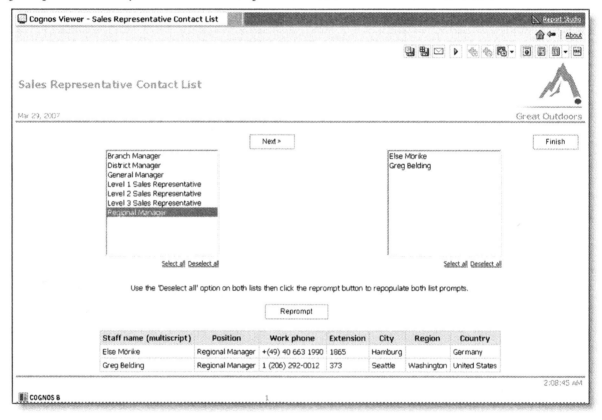

Report Name: Union Crosstab

Cognos report description

"The report is an example of tabular table, which joins to create a complex crosstab. "

What is interesting about this report?

- The use of a text prompt to create a calculated summary column.

- The use of a dynamically calculated column based on a prompt value.

Location

In folder: Public Folders > GO Sales and Retailers > Report Studio Report Samples

Parameter Page

The first page is a customized prompt page with a text prompt. The value of the prompt will be used in the report calculation.

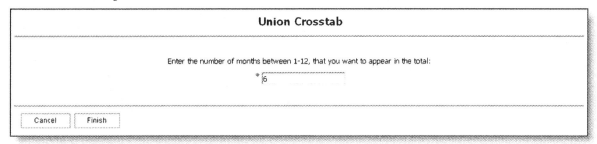

Report Pages

The report shows the monthly total for a year and a dynamically configured column with totals for provided months.

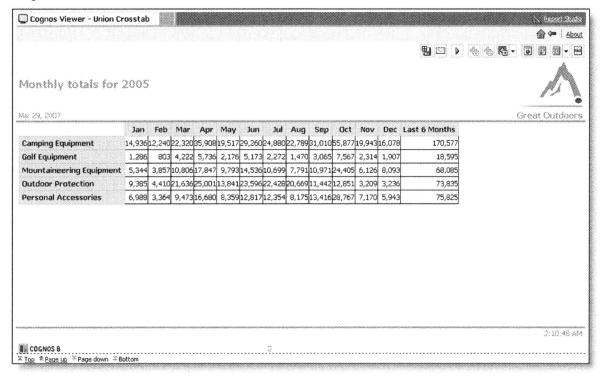

	Jan	Feb	Mar	Apr	May	Jun	Jul	Aug	Sep	Oct	Nov	Dec	Last 6 Months
Camping Equipment	14,936	12,240	22,320	35,908	19,517	29,260	24,880	22,789	31,010	55,877	19,943	16,078	170,577
Golf Equipment	1,286	803	4,222	5,736	2,176	5,173	2,272	1,470	3,065	7,567	2,314	1,907	18,595
Mountaineering Equipment	5,344	3,857	10,806	17,847	9,793	14,536	10,699	7,791	10,971	24,405	6,126	8,093	68,085
Outdoor Protection	9,385	4,410	21,636	25,001	13,841	23,596	22,428	20,669	11,442	12,851	3,209	3,236	73,835
Personal Accessories	6,988	3,364	9,473	16,680	8,359	12,817	12,354	8,175	13,416	28,767	7,170	5,943	75,825

Report Name: Waterfall Chart

Cognos report description

"The Waterfall and Pareto charts are used in combination with a Crosstab to show various metrics. Hover your mouse over Product line to see Product line images."

What is interesting about this report?

- Use of multiple report objects in the same report page. There are two new types of charts shown: Pareto and Waterfall. The Pareto chart shows the cumulative total of the series values, while the Waterfall chart shows the increases of the values in the series.

Location

In folder: Public Folders > GO Sales and Retailers > Report Studio Report Samples

Report Pages

The report shows multiple objects, including a crosstab and charts, in the same page.

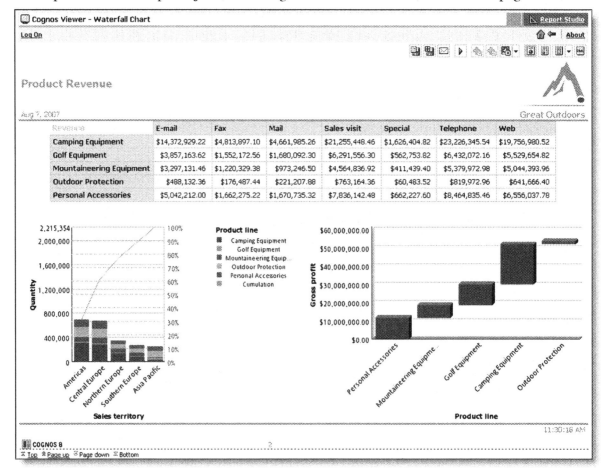

Great Outdoors Company

Reports available at the Great Outdoors Company package.

Reports Included

The following reports contained at the Great Outdoors Company package contain useful features:

- Margins and Revenue Map for United States
- Revenue by Product Line
- Sales Territory Map

Report Name: Margins and Revenue Map for United States

Cognos report description

"This map report shows revenue and margins for each sales branch in the United States."

What is interesting about this report?

- The use of maps to display data. In this case, the report uses points based on colors and size to display values for main cities.

Location

In folder: Public Folders > Great Outdoors Company > Report Studio Report Samples

Report Pages

The report shows the United States map with points showing margin and revenue details for main US cities (based on data for a fictional company).

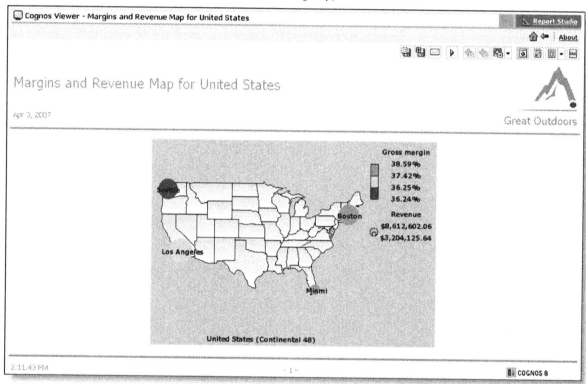

Report Name: Revenue by Product Line

Cognos report description

"This report uses conditional formatting to highlight revenue. You can also drill through to an Analysis Studio report."

What is interesting about this report?

- The dynamic drill-through capabilities of the report.

Location

In folder: Public Folders > Great Outdoors Company > Report Studio Report Samples

Report Pages

The report shows values by Product Line.

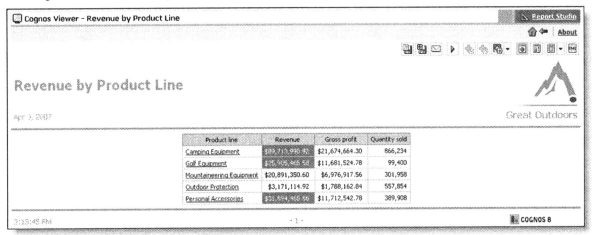

If you select any Product Line hyperlink, it will automatically show you the following report.

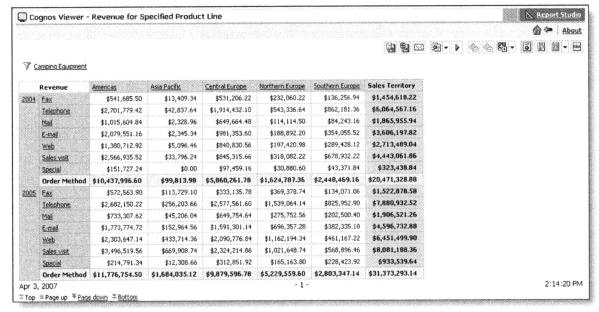

Report Name: Sales Territory Map

Cognos report description

"This report uses a map-style chart to show revenue by sales territory. You can drill through to different reports in Report Studio."

What is interesting about this report?

- The use of maps to display data. In this case, the report uses colors to designate a country or region's revenues by sales territories.

Location

In folder: Public Folders > Great Outdoors Company > Report Studio Report Samples

Report Pages

The report shows the map of the World, with Sales Territories in color based on revenue.

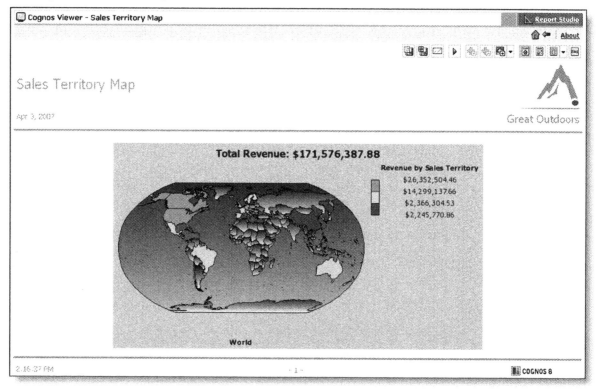

In some spots, you can drill down to a more detailed map.

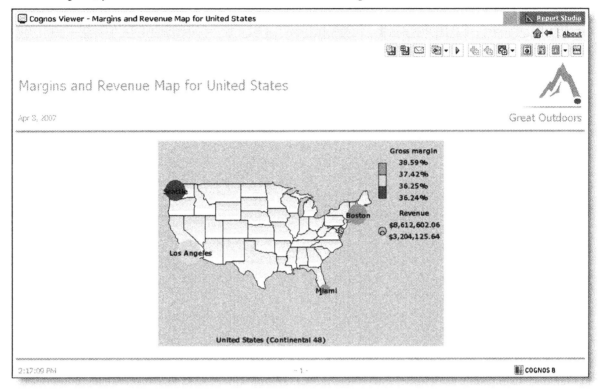

In others, you can drill down for detailed data.

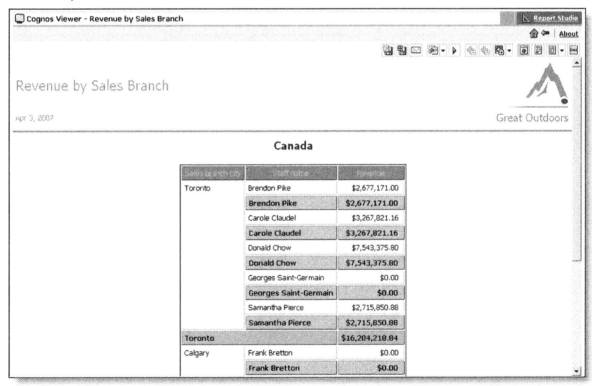

GO Sales

Reports available at the GO Sales package.

Reports Included

The following reports within the GO Sales package contain features of interest:

- Custom Legend
- Product Report
- Retailer Report (Multiple Prompt Values)
- Top 5 Sales Staff

Report Name: Custom Legend

Cognos report description

"The report shows that the legend can be customized in a similar way to the titles."

What is interesting about this report?

- The use of custom legends and color schemes to present information.

Location

In folder: Public Folders > GO Sales > Report Studio Report Samples

Report Pages

The report shows two charts with customized backgrounds and legends.

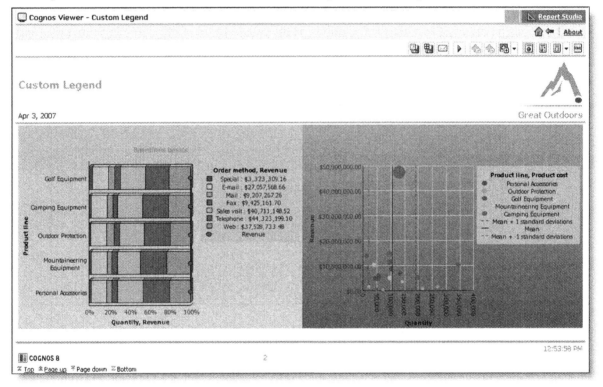

Report Name: Product Report

Cognos report description

"The report displays combination charts with drill through options."

What is interesting about this report?

- The use of complex charts, such as the combination chart shown on the right side. The combination chart combines different types of charts into a single display.

Location

In folder: Public Folders > GO Sales > Report Studio Report Samples

Report Pages

The report shows two highly detailed charts on the same page.

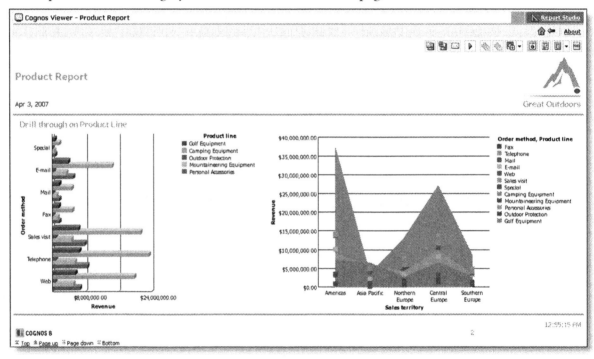

Report Name: Retailer Report (Multiple Prompt Values)

Cognos report description

"This list report accepts multiple prompt values."

What is interesting about this report?

- The use of special charts, such as gauges, to present data visually.

Location

In folder: Public Folders > GO Sales > Report Studio Report Samples

Report Pages

The report shows a list of data with a gauge chart for each specific territory.

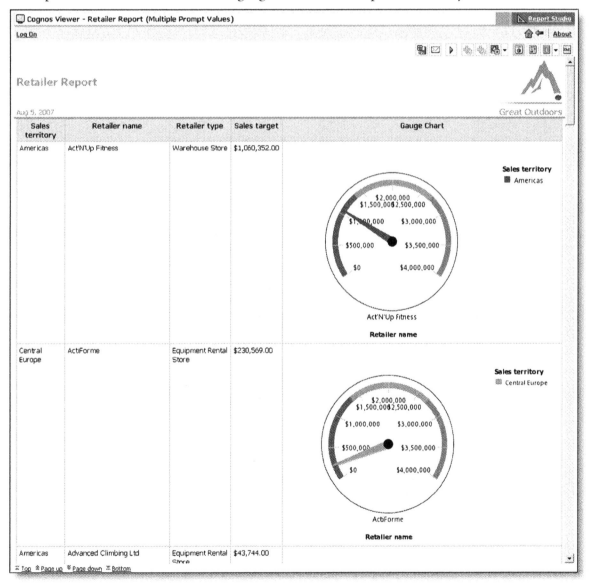

Report Name: Top 5 Sales Staff

Cognos report description

"This list report embeds a bar chart that shows the top five sales representatives by sales targets and revenue."

What is interesting about this report?

- The inclusion of charts into lists of data.

Location

In folder: Public Folders > GO Sales > Report Studio Report Samples

Report Pages

The report shows the top five sales staff with charts displaying their performance.

Index